The Journey Home

Published by Purpose Research, LLC
Charlottesville, Virginia USA
PurposeResearch.com

Cover design, front cover picture, index, and book block layout
©℗2009 Purpose Research; All rights reserved.

Back cover picture ©2009 Jane Roper photography
Picture of Kay (page 85) courtesy of the family of Kay

The author is grateful for permission to include the following previously
copyrighted material:

Gibran, Kahlil, *The Prophet*, pp. 80-81. New York: Alfred A.
Knopf, 1970. Reprinted with permission of Gibran National
Committee, P.O. Box 116-5375, Beirut, Lebanon; Phone & Fax:
(+961-1) 396916; E-mail: k.gibran@cyberia.net.lb.

Martin, Ernest, "The Last Days of Chester Buck" excerpted from
Imagine That! Breaking through to Other Worlds, *Chrysalis
Reader,* vol. 14, West Chester, PA: Swedenborg Foundation
Publishers, 2007.

Acknowledgement of other copyrighted material can be found on pages
111-112.

Soft cover edition
ISBN 978–0–9824278–5–9

First edition

9 8 7 6 5 4 3 2

Preparing for Life's
Ultimate Adventure

The Journey Home

Ann V. Graber

urpose
Research
Charlottesville, Virginia

Also by Ann V. Graber:

Viktor Frankl's Logotherapy

Dedication

To my Guiding Lights

and

To Kay
With love and gratitude
for making an impact on the
lives her spirit touched.

May *The Journey Home* speak to the seeker who
is earnestly looking to expand his or her understanding of the meaning and goal of life—here and in
dimensions beyond.

In Appreciation

To my dear family and friends,
who have stood by me in times of
tribulation and celebration,
my deepest gratitude and love flows out to you.

A book that has been in the making for 25 years, if not longer, has been enriched by many sources, named and unnamed. Beyond those officially acknowledged and referenced in the bibliography, I would like to express my heartfelt gratitude to family, friends and colleagues, students and clients, whose specific contributions are featured in the text:

- Irmeli Sjölie, for providing the vivid Norwegian folklore description of "dying in the olden days."
- Fiona Cartmell, from Scotland, for her moving rendition of providing "medical ministry" to the dying through anointing with aromatherapy.
- Roberto Rodrigues, MD, PhD, from Brazil, for sharing "The Mystery of Your Life" discussion he uses with his patients.
- Hinabaniku, wherever she may be, for her vivid rendition about grieving "New Guinea style."
- Rachel Rivers, DMin, for her insightful reflections on "Spirituality" and for sharing her treasured family memoir of "The Last Days of Chester Buck," that was preserved for posterity by The Rev. Ernest Martin in "Imagine That!" (*A Chrysalis Reader*, 2007).

- Jane Roper, who wrote about "A Powerful Dream" she had of her deceased dad and who contributed the picture on the back cover.
- Betsy Williams, PsyD, who encountered a remarkable attitude in a dying patient as a novice chaplain.
- Nicki Peterson, who movingly described an event that brought about an outpouring of spontaneous grief and respect in a tragic and sudden death.
- Vicki Stumpf, for keeping us supplied with kuchen on special occasions.

৪৩

The memoir, *Kay's Legacy*, was made possible through the first person accounts of her children Steve, Evelyn, Mike, and Brian Peterson, as well as extended family and friends.

Special recognition for their testimonials, which are included in the text, is extended to Audrey Schlote, Ken Westermann, Marion and John Commerford, Phyllis Ferris, and Michael Peterson.

The dear people of the Garden Chapel, particularly The Rev. David Rienstra, his wife Carole Rienstra, Marty Mason, David Currall, Carolyn Bower, and others who enthusiastically took on Kay's Memorial Garden project and made it a reality, deserve a heartfelt "Thank You!"

Sincere appreciation is extended to all who participated in *Kay's Legacy* in significant ways, and who helped make her journey home an inspiring event for many.

Father Jerry Murasso's thoughtful gift of the decorative plaque with the Prayer of St. Francis, from Assisi, Italy, was received with deep gratitude and awe about its timeliness.

Contents

Prologue

The unexamined life is not worth living.
Socrates

This book has been in the making for a long time, perhaps all of my life. Having been a serious child, I became an introspective young adult, and in time—I would like to think—grew into a perceptive mature adult. Given this natural predilection, I experienced life more from an inner-directed vantage point. This view offered insights along the journey of life and led to the exploration of dimensions of reality that seemed veiled to my more outer-directed companions along the way.

Encouraged by friends and colleagues who believe that our times demand deeper exploration and understanding of dimensions beyond logic, I offer my impressions about dying in this book. It presents an awareness that death is a natural occurrence on our journey of becoming. My perceptions were gathered in the "school of life," by reflecting on what the way-showers of humanity have taught and by listening to others who bravely faced their uncertainties about dying and needed an empathetic ear.

The book begins with a personal numinous experience, the insights gained from it, and the mandate the occurrence brought with it: to help lessen the fear of death rampant in our materialistic and extroverted culture.

Helpful suggestions will be offered to assist those who are facing their ultimate fears, and need to make preparations to go to their rest in spite of them. We will look at how others have described the transformative process of going from fear of death to acceptance of it, leading to a peaceful transition. Among nonthreatening ways to facilitate such transformation of attitudes, beyond the rites and rituals available to a person from their religious faith, are: attuning to nature, imagery, stories, art, music, and whatever helps one to cultivate an inner peace in which fears melt away.

Reminiscences, life reviews, and life previews allow us to explore areas where reconciliation needs to take place, forgiveness extended, and gratitude expressed. There is great comfort in knowing that one's life can be brought to a harmonious ending. It engenders hope that one's life has been worthwhile and that the accumulated wisdom, harvested from life experiences, will live on.

Some of the material contained in this discussion has been presented at professional conferences; other segments have been published in various venues, albeit in a more scholarly format. This book is an attempt to write from the heart and soul. It is intended to speak simply to anyone who courageously contemplates the inevitability of his or her own death and the implications surrounding it. Those attending the dying will be helped to understand a dying person's process with an insider's view, along with some practiced know-how.

The final chapter depicts a memorable example of one valiant person's conscious preparation for her approaching death. *Kay's Legacy* is a testimonial—told by those who participated in her life and were present at her transition. It demonstrates that death need not be feared, but anticipated as the ultimate adventure awaiting us at the end of our mortal journey.

May you find comfort—even exhilaration—in discovering that our walk on Earth is only a step in the eternal expansion of consciousness. As we allow our highest truths and values to guide us in everything we do, awareness will shift unendingly: beginning with rather dense and crude sensations in physical form, to ever-subtler sensitivities and experiences in dimensions beyond. In that context, death of our physical bodies can be likened to a commencement exercise that we pass through as we journey homeward.

1. Adventure Inward

Oh death, where is thy sting?
1 Corinthians 15:55

Although I had believed in life beyond death since childhood, it was largely a matter of faith. Faith became knowing when a window to another dimension, or plane of awareness, flew open for me one day. On that eventful day, my life changed dramatically, both internally and externally.

On a vacation trip a year earlier, I had been involved in an automobile accident. The rear-end collision had resulted in an undetected injury to my neck, which caused discomfort and increasing numbness of my left arm and hand, particularly when I was at work, typing medical transcription. I found I could relieve the pain and pressure in my neck by dangling my head over the edge of the bed. This is what I was doing on that fateful morning when I slid off the bed and landed on the back of my neck. As my body hit the floor, I felt an excruciating pain, as if my spinal cord had been cut by a knife. This was followed by a lightning-like sensation surging down my spine and exiting through every nerve ending. Then... nothing. No sensation, no movement! I lay crumpled on the floor, the way I had fallen, and could not move. Gradually the realization dawned on me: "*I am paralyzed!*"

1

Following the shock of this horrific discovery, I began to assess my situation. As a former anatomy/physiology instructor I had enough medical knowledge to conclude that I had sustained a traumatic spinal cord injury with loss of function and sensation below the neck, and was quadriplegic. I also knew that at the prevailing level of medical technology, we simply didn't know how to mend mangled spinal cords. Since I could still breathe unassisted, I deduced that the lesion must be below C–3, the third cervical vertebra.

I was fully conscious and painfully aware of my predicament. The accident took place around 7:30 on a Monday morning. Everyone had left for the day. I was alone. No one was expected to be back before evening. Fears, couched in questions and answers, assailed me: Will I still be alive by then? It won't matter! Who wants to live in a body that doesn't function? And my worst fear of all: What if I was comatose and could not object to being kept alive through mechanical means? The horror of that possibility engulfed me along with a wave of self pity. What awful fate had befallen me!

Then some aspect from deep within stepped forth and took charge as if to say, "Stop your sniveling! This is not the time to feel sorry for your self. Use what little time you have left to put your inner house in order!" It was as if the CEO of my intrapsychic board of regents had spoken. This appeared to be a sensible suggestion. I was surprised to learn that my emotions did not have to run the show, that a higher wisdom could be in charge. Heeding its directive, I had to acknowledge that I was probably about to die. How would I prepare to die—consciously—not some day when I'm old, but now, probably in the next few hours?

As my bodily functions and sensations diminished, perceptions became keener. Never before, nor since, have

I been able to think so clearly and rapidly. It was as if
the central nervous system was an organ through which
the mind operates on the physical plane. Now the veil of
matter was lifting and I had direct access to my mind,
unencumbered by limiting neural pathways. I perceived
myself more and more from outside of my bodily confines.
It felt as if my life force was being withdrawn through
the crown of my head and was gathering above me. This
process took several hours. I became the observer and
the observed. For instance, I had landed in a heap with
my weight compressing my left leg. I could dispassion-
ately observe that the circulation was cut off in the leg. I
watched it turn pale, then waxen looking, as if belonging
to a corpse. All at the same time, I felt deep sadness for
my leg, as well as boundless gratitude for its having
carried me through life, along with the joy of dancing
and skiing on it. In this expanded reality, everything was
happening simultaneously with great intensity. It was
trans-temporal: I was in linear time as well as beyond it.

The thought occurred to me to do a "general confes-
sion with an act of contrition" as I had been taught in
my Catholic childhood: to ask for forgiveness for having
wronged anyone or having harbored resentment. As soon
as I had that intention clearly formulated, my memory
banks opened up in a way I had never experienced before.
Suddenly I had access to past experiences in a multi-
sensory way. I not only saw the events of my life pass
before me, but sensed the wider implications of every act
in a holographic progression. I was acutely aware of how
I and others felt simultaneously. For example, I knew
each and every child in my first grade class again. I could
clearly see the wispy pig tails of the little girl in front of
me, and was fascinated by the intricate Norwegian design
of a boy's sweater. I was hearing the teacher's voice while

knowing what impression he had made on each of us, far beyond the lessons we had studied in class. And so it went through the many days and years of my life. I was amazed at the mental acuity at my disposal. Everything I had ever learned was stored knowledge available to me, in glorious color and sound, complete with feelings accompanied by smells and tastes. It was incredible—a hologram of my personal life journey!

When I reached the end of my life review, a dizzying perceptual ride through several decades, I felt great relief. I saw it as a life rich in meaningful experiences: some joyful, some painful, but an eventful life with many challenges and opportunities for soul growth. There were some unhealed relationships into which I poured all the love and goodwill at my disposal, trusting that my intentionality would direct it to its destination.

Then I began to say my good-byes. This was truly wrenching, as I was very much attached to the people I loved. With deep love and caring I took my leave from those near and dear to me. As the circle of love expanded, I was amazed to see how many people had influenced my life and made their contributions. I began to understand how interconnected we all are. At that moment, it was easy to love the whole world and everybody in it.

Gradually I reached a point of relinquishment where I concluded it was a good life! If I had to do it over, I probably wouldn't do any better. This was very comforting. A tranquility and stillness began to permeate my entire being. I was at peace. All fear of death had vanished. The sun was high on the horizon now. My breathing was shallow and labored. Death would be a welcome visitor. My last conscious thought was, "Into your hands I commend my spirit, oh Lord!"

છ

What I am about to relate next needs to be prefaced. No one says it better than the seer into other dimensions, Emanuel Swedenborg, when he describes spirit slipping into a stillness at death, rather like falling asleep, and experiencing inexpressible Divine things of infinite wisdom; of seeing countless things, of which not even a ten-thousandth part could be described in human words because they would not fit into concepts that have matter-centered content.

After having surrendered my life into the Lord's keeping, the scene shifted. Awareness of the room where I lay on the floor faded. I was somewhere else! Trying to orient myself to my surroundings, I perceived myself as being out in deep space. Far below, I could see our beautiful planet, the Earth, glistening and turning gracefully. I sensed that I was not alone. There were presences about me, very benevolent beings. I did not perceive them as having form, but they were identifiable by their inner qualities, which radiated from them and permeated the realm, giving it a shimmering glow. It was a wondrous place, a state of being. I was on hallowed ground. My impression was of swirling currents of pure compassion, of radiant love, of infinite wisdom, of aliveness and vitality that sustained worlds without end. These qualities were as palpable as tangible objects are in our world, not abstract or elusive. I felt wondrously safe there. I was *home*!

I also felt warmly welcomed and was given to understand that my life's learning tasks were completed. What joy! The thought of spending eternity in that awesome realm of existence filled me with an ecstasy that is unimaginable where I had come from.

Then a drama was staged for my edification: Our world was shown to me. It had points of Light as well as places of darkness. There were many changes occurring rapidly all around the planet Earth. This appeared to me as energy vortices twirling, picking up momentum, colliding with others, changing direction and velocity, regrouping and reforming, gradually learning to cooperate for the benefit of all—until eventually they moved with grace and beauty, in harmony with one another. The implication was: There is, and there will be, much chaotic whirling of energies about the planet Earth. Souls are needed there who can be stable elements, points of stillness, while the winds of change and transformation blow about. I intuited an invitation, "Will you be one of them?"

What? Go back into that crumpled body that's beyond repair? I didn't want to leave that wondrously shimmering realm, nor the company of those magnificent beings! But it was not polite to say *"no"* to God or to His Emissaries, was it? So I gave my consent to return for an extended tour on planet Earth. Mine would be a bit part in the supportive cast that could be played, if need be, from a wheelchair.

No more than I had given my consent to return, when I became conscious of being on the floor in my room again. The door was being opened. Against all odds, someone came by at noon and found me. I was rushed to a hospital that specialized in treating spinal cord injuries. After many months in traction, a spinal fusion, rehabilitation, the ministrations of many kinds of healers, and the loving support of kindred spirits, my recovery exceeded the most optimistic medical prognosis. Although handicapped, I have left the life I once knew—and my wheelchair—behind.

∞

Has looking through that window beyond finite consciousness made a difference in my life? The first and most immediate change was in my attitude regarding death. If I believed in life after death before, now I *know* that personal consciousness lives on. Moreover, I had experienced the transition from three-dimensional to multidimensional reality. Death will be an adventure to be looked forward to, not an event to be feared, when this "tour of duty" is successfully completed.

I now live with a greater sense of vocation, knowing that each of us has a life purpose to fulfill, to do that which is most meaningful at a given time and circumstance. We are to respond to the demands life places upon us, and meet its challenges to the best of our ability, by making wise choices and carrying them out. Thereby we co-create who we ultimately become. Life is a gift, not a given. Each of us plays a part in the symphony of life. The orchestra of planet Earth is practicing its Hymn to the Universe. There may still be discordant notes to be heard, but we are getting more attuned to each other and to the Conductor. It will be a glorious sound when everyone knows and plays his or her part in concert with others.

Since that glimpse into another dimension of reality, indeed, there has been much swirling of energies about the planet. Awareness has shifted and consciousness has expanded in many ways. Collisions of thought streams and belief systems were and are inevitable until we acquire a cooperative, instead of a competitive, approach. As more and more of us access that greater reality within, fear will lessen—not only the fear of death, but also the fear of each other. Then bridges of trust can be built, and we will walk toward the future together, in harmony.

It became obvious to me that experiences beyond finite reality are not the purview of a select few, but the common destiny and heritage of humankind. Excursions beyond finite existence into domains of expanded reality are our birthright. There have been, and still are, spiritual giants among us who have pointed the way. At the core of their message we find Love, Beauty, and Goodness—endeavoring to expand our consciousness toward greater wisdom.

As windows of awareness open, and our perceptual boundaries expand, let us not erect new ones by seeking validation for our own inner experiences through conformity with the insightful experiences of others. The divine spark in each individual is unique; therefore, the profound experiences of each one of us are valid. Conveying the sacred and infinite through finite language is difficult, if not impossible. The peripheral details of these experiences vary according to individual perceptions. Their interpretation of meaning content will further be colored by personal understanding and cultural idiom.

Just as the description of my experience is uniquely mine, so are the descriptions of others' experiences uniquely theirs. I tend to take these accounts less literally than I once did, but look for the spirit contained in the message. What emerges is:

> *There is a wondrous life to be lived,*
> *here and beyond,*
> *as we love and serve each other!*

My own experience in that state of expanded awareness implied a mandate: to help others understand that death is not to be feared, but viewed as an integral part of mortal life. Death is but the natural ending of mortal existence when our learning objectives have been met, when our physical vehicles and time allotment have become exhausted. Then it is time for our indwelling spirit to journey home, taking the wisdom harvested from life experiences with it.

Preparing for that journey homeward with forethought—before we are at death's door—will directly impact the quality of life we lead. Keeping in mind the transitoriness of life in physical form, we will want to make choices that ennoble, not debase, our human spirit during our lifetime.

That visionary theologian and scientist of the twentieth century, Pierre Teilhard de Chardin, resonated with these sentiments beautifully when he succinctly stated:

> *We are not human beings*
> *Having a spiritual experience.*
> *We are spiritual beings*
> *Having a human experience.*

2. Preparing for the Journey Home

To everything there is a season,
and a time to every purpose
under heaven:
A time to be born, and a time to die.
Ecclesiastes 3: 1–2

In our increasingly urban culture, the natural rhythm of life and death is no longer observable as it was in our agrarian past. As we became more and more removed from observing the cycles of nature at close range, we also distanced ourselves from the miracle of birth and the witnessing of death.

A friend from Scandinavia told me that, according to Norwegian folklore, dying used to be a communally accepted part of life. Irmeli Sjölie described the custom surrounding the event as follows:

When Ola became too old or sick to leave his bed,
family, friends, and neighbors would gather outside,
open his windows and begin calling to his soul,
"Come on, Ola, leave your old sick body! Let your
soul fly free! Come on out, Ola, join your friends!"
And, sooner or later, Ola would leave his body and
expire. When the body could no longer sustain life, it
was time to die. That's the way it was done in olden
times.

By contrast, in our contemporary technological society death is an uncomfortable subject. By and large, we treat it as something that must be denied or deferred at all cost. In times of crisis involving death or dying, family and friends may be ill equipped to help, due to their own uncertainty and attendant shock. When the inevitable comes to pass, often professionals—in various secular and religious capacities—are called upon for assistance.

At the time of this writing, it has been reported that 60% of people in the United States die in hospitals, 20% in nursing homes, and only about 20% die at home. We can readily see that we have not only separated ourselves from death and dying, but by relegating the care of the dying to professionals, we have lost the intimacy that accompanies the dying process. At a time when a person may need the ministrations of family and friends the most, he or she is largely separated from them and isolated in an unfamiliar place. By and large, the hospital setting is impersonal. Consequently, when a terminally ill person checks into a hospital, he or she becomes a "patient"—individuality, even personhood, is compromised. There may be help available for alleviating some of the physical symptoms, but where is the care of the soul, of one's uniqueness and individuality?

The phenomenal growth of the hospice movement in recent years provides ample evidence that we are in dire need of help when it comes to end-of-life issues. In part, adjustments in how we approach death were brought about by changes due to industrialization, urbanization, and the mobility of our society. However, one of the biggest causes of our changed attitude toward death is that in earlier times people died faster. People died of acute illnesses or accidental injuries; there were few cures or injury repairs available. Now, only about 10% die sudden deaths; the remaining 90% die more slowly. Many acute illnesses are now curable, while others are treatable as chronic diseases. This has prolonged the process of dying but has not changed the inevitability of death.

The holistic approach employed by hospice addresses the whole person, including physical, psychosocial, and spiritual needs. Respecting the humanity of the dying person and encouraging closeness to family and loved ones removes some of the potential anxiety. Dying at home, wherever possible, is preferable to dying among strangers. As a first step when hospice is invited into the treatment team, the illusion that recovery will be forthcoming has to be given up. Denial of approaching death can no longer be sustained; neither by the patient, nor by the family. Those who can accept this inevitability, in spite of the anguish it may cause, are preparing for a harmonious parting of ways on their journey home.

Home! The very sound of the word evokes in us eternal yearnings for a safe haven, a place of refuge and protection from harm, a place of warmth, comfort, and familiarity. It speaks of love and enduring relationships. For some, it may evoke nostalgia for a place they once knew; for others, a projection toward a heavenly home. For those who come to view dying as a journey home, the powerful attributes of *home* beckon invitingly. The journey, even if painful, is experienced as a return to a longed-for state. Intuitive knowing whispers: "After a long and eventful absence, I am returning to where I came from, enriched by experiences and hopefully wiser. I will no longer be a stranger in a strange world, but a citizen in my own country of Spirit. There I can enjoy the companionship of others of like mind and soul. All is well, I am going home!"

The noted Viennese psychiatrist, Dr. Viktor Frankl, was asked during an interview, "How do you prepare someone to die?"

"I wouldn't venture to prepare anyone else to die, unless I had first prepared myself," replied Dr. Frankl. "My patients know exactly when what I say is authentic and when it is not." Frankl's reply indicates that we must first come to terms with our own mortality in order to be comfortable in the presence of death or those who are dying. This may come from direct experience, from one's faith, or from conscious preparation for the task. Ideally, we would want to live each day as if it could be our last. Then there would be less angst to confront.

∞

The theme of preparing for life's ultimate adventure invariably deals with the great equalizer, death. There is no greater event humanity has in common. Even birth, it can be argued, has its disparity. But, when approaching death, we are all headed for "the great unknown." We have our fears to face and, in spite of them, preparations to make.

To that end, it is helpful to be acquainted with the teachings of luminaries among humankind, past and present. They include revelators of the world's religions as well as philosophers, scientists, poets, and mystics. Some of our heroes may live in stories or fables.

We may have examples in our own family history of peaceful transitions following a life courageously lived with its hardships bravely borne. The lives of "saints" and ordinary decent people abound in accounts of nobility of spirit and fearless deaths. Many of them have insights to

offer that will be helpful in accepting the transitoriness
of our mortal existence.

Victor Hugo, whose writings inspired that symbol of
freedom, the Statue of Liberty, also symbolically described
death and liberation when he wrote "Eternal Spring":

Winter is on my head
But eternal spring is in my heart.
The nearer I approach the end,
The plainer I hear around me
The immortal symphonies
Of the world to come....

&

It is well documented that during a major trauma
or life crisis, particularly if it involves death, people
turn first to their religious leaders for spiritual and
psychological support. Assistance of a religious nature
necessarily implies a religious philosophy and, perhaps,
a method of counseling. Traditionally pastors, priests,
ministers, rabbis, imams, other clergy, chaplains, and
religious individuals have fulfilled this role within their
own congregations and among the adherents of their faith.
It is within their professional and vocational domain to
counsel and guide the faithful.

In recent times, counseling those in distress has
expanded far beyond the province of the clergy. In addition to ministry professionals, lay people are being trained
to provide both pastoral and other types of counseling.
Their outreach is extending far beyond strictly denom-
inational boundaries. The diverse field of counseling
seeks to address psychological needs of persons needing
help, particularly those undergoing traumatic or lasting
changes. Pastoral counseling, for example, is designed to

fill the gap between psychiatric and exclusively religious functions, to assist us during psycho-spiritual crises. It is emerging as a vigorous new branch on the tree of human services.

In our "melting pot" culture of diverse ethnicity and religious plurality, the pastoral counselor, chaplain and other helpers, especially if working in hospitals or other public institutions, will have to understand the urgent needs of those seeking help, particularly when facing death. A counseling philosophy will be required that is ecumenically tolerant and inclusive, not exclusively steeped in one's own faith orientation.

Although this discussion is primarily based on a Christ-centered religious understanding, it includes the wider company of truth seekers, whether they profess to belong to a church or not. The mystic Emanuel Swedenborg reminds us that all members of the human race belong to the Church Universal by virtue of their humanity. However, individual members of humanity may also elect to belong to a Church Specific; ideally, a church or religion that suits their development and furthers their spiritual growth.

∾

In my search for helpful counseling theories that address life and death issues in a meaningful way, the work of Viktor Frankl stands out. He is the author of the classic *Man's Search for Meaning* and many other books that further develop his psychotherapy. Dr. Frankl is comfortable with the thought of our transitoriness. He sees it as part of our human condition that cannot be changed or avoided; it must be *accepted*. This acceptance is not passive, but becomes the motivation, the very incentive, to make the most of life while we have the opportunity to do so. Since we have only limited time available, we must seize the meaning of each moment and live in the present, while looking to the future with hope.

In view of the relative scarcity of psychological theories that come even close to the ideals and visions most major religions hold for humanity, Dr. Frankl's philosophy is refreshingly optimistic, yet pragmatic. Franklian psychology includes the spiritual dimension and honors religious values. It sees the human being reaching for something beyond self, toward "Ultimate Meaning"— God. Frankl (1997) gives us an explanation of what he is alluding to by stating, "God is the partner of your most intimate soliloquies. Whenever you are talking to yourself in utmost sincerity and ultimate solitude—he to whom you are addressing yourself may justifiably be called God." Frankl notes that a religious person would assert that these are real dialogues between himself and God, while an atheist would be equally correct in insisting that they are only monologues within his own mind. Neither would dispute the presence of *Geist* (the nucleus of personality) in such a dialogue.

Although Dr. Frankl tries very hard to stay on the scientific side of the fence that divides psychiatry and religion, he is obviously a man of deep faith, which is reflected in his counseling theory and its application. Franklian psychology looks for what is meaningful in a person's life, what is of value to an individual. Based on that, meaning-centered interventions can be offered when troubling life situations arise. Frankl maintains that our primary motivation in life is *meaning*—that which gives reason for being. We may have drives for pleasure and power, but we are innately meaning-oriented beings. The main tenets of his theory can be briefly summarized as follows:

- We have the *freedom of will* (within obvious biological, sociological, even psychological limitations) to fulfill the meaning of our lives. By our choices and subsequent actions we determine who we ultimately become.
- The *will to meaning* is the primary motivation for living. We are fulfilled (find contentment and happiness) when we know we are doing what is ours to do in life; when we choose what *ought to be* over what *is*.
- *Life has meaning under all circumstances* (even the most miserable ones). It is our responsibility to respond to life's demands to the best of our ability, moment by moment.

This is a lofty, yet commonsense approach to life. It sees value even in suffering. When suffering is unavoidable, and we endure it courageously, it can become the crucible for heightening our sensitivity, refining our humanness, and escalating our spiritual growth. We can emerge from our trials transformed into stronger and more compassionate human beings.

There is common ground upon which religion and Franklian psychology are standing: *spirituality*. Religions may value spirituality for different reasons than does Frankl's psychotherapy, but both recognize that spirituality is the bedrock upon which their systems are founded. This is true whether the belief system of a given religion is aiming for salvation of the soul or a therapeutic system is designed to heal the human psyche.

What is spirituality? In *World Spirituality: An Encyclopedic History of the Religious Quest*, Ewert Cousins points out that spirituality should be distinguished from theology and the study of religion. The inner dimension of the person is called "the spirit" by certain traditions.

This spiritual core is the deepest center of the person. It is here that the person is open to a transcendent dimension; it is here that the person experiences ultimate reality. Reflecting on that, I came to understand that spirituality is an inherent part of being human; it is the essential core of a human being; it is the indwelling *theos* [Greek: God]. *Theo-logy,* then, becomes the study of that indwelling God, the Ground of our Being. It is also the study of our relationship to theos, God personified in theistic religions.

Throughout history, we have wondered about our origin and our destiny. We have a deep innate yearning to belong, to feel connected to that mysterious source, to understand our reason for being. Ideas about the Creator and the universe, as well as beliefs concerning our place in it, have emerged in answer to these yearnings. Over time, rituals were developed, which were intended to bring believers closer to this mysterious source and to establish union with it and community with others. We call these belief systems with their attendant rituals *religions*. Religions assist their adherents to reach toward God according to a particular understanding of God. It follows then, that *spirituality is innate* and that *religion is acquired*. People may change their religion, but they retain their inherent spirituality. Consequently, we can view the interconnectedness of these concepts as follows:

- ◆ *theology* as study about God;
- ◆ *religion* as a path to God, the Source of Being;
- ◆ *spirituality* as that essential human endowment in which direct experience of God can take place.

❀

When a valued friend and pastor, Dr. Rachel Rivers, was asked to define spirituality, she began by quoting His Holiness the Dalai Lama, who writes about spirituality as "the full richness and simple wholesomeness of our basic human values." Stating that this rang true to her, she then proceeded to give further definitions of spirituality that "bubbled up" inside her. Here are some of her gems:

- Spirituality is composed of loving kindness, peace, hope, joy, integrity, respect, justice, compassion, honor, goodwill, creativity, wholeness, courage, honesty, equality, harmony, unity, patience, delight.
- Spirituality is ineffable, but it is made visible in goodness, truth, and beauty.
- Spirituality is love in action.

These definitions speak of what the Dalai Lama referred to as "the wholesomeness of our basic human values." It is helpful to keep in mind that every person has a spiritual core where that fire inside of us resides. How this spiritual fire is actualized or how it is put to use determines what kind of person we become. In that sense, we are co-creators of ourselves and of our destiny.

There are many paths leading to deeper understanding: they may be religious or nonreligious, theistic or nontheistic in their understanding of the Source of Being. The transformative process will take on a hopeful note if it is accepted as a presupposition that *spirituality is central*, and that a person's particular *religion is supplemental*.

∞

Regardless of our role, whether we are a professional, a lay helper or volunteer, a friend or family member, we need to be attitudinally ready before we attempt to help others face their fear of dying. We need to be at peace with the inevitability of death—our own and the death of others. My own fear of death dissolved when I experienced a shift in consciousness from our three-dimensional to a multidimensional reality during my adventure inward. However, this is not the only way to reach an attitude of acceptance and peace regarding death.

Transforming our attitude toward death—from fear to acceptance, even to anticipation of greater things to come—has been addressed by theologians, insightful philosophers and self-transcending psychotherapists. The voice of the poet, Kahlil Gibran (1970), also speaks to us on the topic. The windows of his soul seem to have been wide open to Spirit's whisperings when he wrote *The Prophet* in 1923. At that time, he was a young man, yet the wisdom he expressed through his Prophet seems timeless. This is what he had to say on death:

> *If you would indeed behold the spirit of death,*
> *open your heart wide unto the body of life.*
> *For life and death are one,*
> *even as the river and the sea are one....*
> *Your fear of death is but the trembling of the*
> *shepherd when he stands before the king*
> *whose hand is to be laid upon him in honor.*

3. Journeying with Others

Where two or three
are gathered together in my name,
there am I
in the midst of them.
Matthew 18:20

Even if it is not explicitly stated, this presence is implicitly invited by the intention to honor the innate spirit of God in each other. "Only union *through* love and *in* love (using the word 'love' in its widest and most real sense of 'mutual internal affinity')... brings individuals together, not superficially and tangentially but center to center," writes Teilhard de Chardin in *The Future of Man*. The perceptible flow of grace that occurs when such center-to-center union can be established is truly transformative. The transcendental quality of such an encounter may well be attributed to the presence of the universal God being "in the midst of them."

Beyond being well intentioned, even steeped in our own faith, it is helpful for anyone wishing to be of service to those who are dying to have some rudimentary understanding of their needs. This discussion will focus on the psycho-spiritual needs, beyond the obvious physical needs. It will speak particularly to the stage in life in which a cure is no longer likely, but comfort measures can be provided; when all efforts to restore health have been exhausted, and the approaching death has to be faced.

However, let us not wait until such a time, but prepare for the inevitable transition with forethought while we are able to reflect on it, and anticipate the needs that may arise. Not only the outer necessities, but also the inner, less discernible, longings need to be addressed.

∞

The field of human services is an intuitive art, as well as a learned craft. The counselor or helper walks a fine line. If the craft is overdeveloped to the exclusion of the art, there is danger of it becoming rote by only using standardized formulations. Conversely, if the art of the counseling process is overemphasized, it may become vague and directionless. Therefore, heart and head must walk hand-in-hand for genuine and lasting progress to be made.

At times, the head may have to lead; at other times, the heart. If the head predominates, not only compassion, but also insight and intuition about the uniqueness of the individual, may be lost. When we allow the heart to lead, we can say with Pascal, "The heart has its reasons, which reason does not know."

Not all are comfortable or prepared to enter into the intensity of the dying person's journey. During the preparatory stages leading to acceptance of life's transitoriness, the critically ill person may well be—psychologically speaking—thrashing about wildly. To work with the dying requires a certain maturity. We are forced to take a good hard look at our own attitude toward death and dying before we can sit quietly and calmly with a terminally ill person. When a meeting of two people, who can be present without fear and anxiety, occurs, a gateway is formed that leads to genuine communication. Whoever undertakes this role, whether a therapist, doctor, chaplain, friend, or family member, will need to let the individual know by words or actions that he or she is not going to run away if the word *cancer* or *dying* is mentioned.

ᚪ

Medical science has, in broad strokes, mapped out the accompanying psychological stages attendant to the physical decline during the dying process. The pioneering work of Dr. Elisabeth Kübler-Ross on death and dying, followed by the work of others, brought to light much helpful information about the attitudes that accompany varying stages during the transition process. Except in cases of sudden death, these stages of shifting attitudes are generally recognizable. The intensity and duration of a prevailing attitude may differ, but there is a definite progression observable in coming to terms with one's mortality. It behooves us to be knowledgeable about this process, especially when attending those who are approaching death or when comforting their loved ones.

After years of research, pursued through conversations with dying patients and interviews with their families, Kübler-Ross published her findings in the landmark book, *On Death and Dying.* She identified distinctive transitional stages in transforming one's attitude, from fear of death to acceptance of it. A brief summary of these characteristic changes can serve as a guide when dealing with our own conscious reflections on death, or when assisting someone to prepare for the transition.

Denial
When the awareness of a terminal illness first presents itself, the person usually reacts with shock. This

temporary state of shock with its accompanying numbness gradually gives way to *denial*, which says, "No, not me, it cannot be true." This tends to be the case whether a poor prognosis is presented directly to the patient or whether this conclusion is reached by the patient independently. The initial reaction to facing one's own impending death is shock and denial. This is particularly true for persons in young adulthood through middle age when ties to life, family, and young children are the strongest.

Denial of the seriousness of declining health may lead to an isolation which is either self-imposed or related to shock and reactions experienced by family members. Few people will remain in denial until the end. The isolation can be used to find strength to cope with the situation and to come to terms with the inevitable.

Anger

When denial cannot be maintained any longer, it is often followed by feelings of *anger*, which include rage, envy, and resentment. The question now becomes: "Why me?" This stage is more difficult to cope with than the stage of denial. Anger may be displaced upon family and caregivers or randomly on the environment, which makes interactions with others painful. Since people tend to keep their distance from someone who is angry, the isolation of the dying person increases.

It is essential that a patient's support network is made aware that anger (within limits) is a natural part of the process of letting go. Anger serves a function in that it temporarily serves to make the situation more tolerable for the patient. If it can be understood by family, caregivers, and friends that these manifestations of anger are part of a suffering person's adaptive mechanism and are not to be taken personally, then the patient's anger becomes easier to endure.

Bargaining

This stage is less well recognized, but vitally important to the process. If denial has not worked, and anger has not brought about the desired result, *bargaining* frequently occurs. This can take many forms, such as pleading for heroic measures or experimental medical treatments, searching for elusive "cures" elsewhere, or pleading with God and bargaining with Him, offering anything in return for His divine favor—if He will only take away this fate.

This is the stage in a person's life reminiscent of the prayer vigil of Jesus in the Garden of Gethsemane when he prayed, "O, my Father, if it be possible, let this cup pass from me" (Matthew 26:39). There may be much agony before a person's prayer can be concluded with, "Not my will, but Thy will be done."

Depression

When the terminally ill person cannot deny the mounting evidence of increasing physical and emotional symptoms (e.g., weakness and helplessness) any longer, when anger and bargaining have not changed circumstances, there comes a time when a sense of great loss is experienced. Loss of health predictably will lead to other losses: loss of lifestyle, inability to work, financial losses, loss of meaningful activities and involvement in life, loss of friends and associates, or loss of independence. As helplessness increases there may be a feeling of loss of dignity. Any of these losses may manifest as *depression*. This stage of depression can be minimized through supportive interventions and understanding of a person's needs by family and others.

There is another stage of depression, however, in which encouragement from others, that things will get better, is misguided. This stage of depression deals with preparatory grief. If the first stage of depression can be considered *reactive depression*, the latter is a *preparatory depression*. The first is quite different in nature from the second. The preparatory stage may be the time when a spiritually attuned helper can be of most help.

The preparatory grief stage is a very important time on the journey. Here, "man's adversity is God's opportunity." This phase has little to do with reactions to past losses, but with preparation for impending losses. This is not the time to try to cheer up the depressed person, but to allow and assist him or her to make necessary preparations for the departure. This is the time to put one's house in order—to bring closure to the business of one's life, to make peace, and to bid farewell to those who are near and dear. It is also time to make preparations to account for the life one has lived and will soon be leaving behind.

Acceptance

If a person has progressed through the previously encountered stages, there will come a time when there is neither depression nor anger about one's fate. The individual, who has been able to express and deal with feelings as they arose, has mourned both past and impending losses, and has been able to put worldly affairs in order and complete meaningful tasks, will next reach a stage of *acceptance*. This person will begin to contemplate the coming transition with a degree of quiet expectancy.

The acceptance stage should not be mistaken for an overtly happy time. It can be almost devoid of feeling.

It is as if pain had gone, the struggle is over, and there comes a time for the final rest before the long journey. With acceptance there comes a turning inward, often characterized by increased need for sleep. Interest in outer things diminishes. Visitors often are not desired. Verbal communication becomes minimal. Silence is welcome. A gentle holding of hands, a look, a touch are the most meaningful communications at this time. The transition is near.

It is important to note that these stages may not occur in the orderly delineation described here, but may be intermingled. The helper needs to remember to be present to the individual's unique process, to gently guide the course, but not to impose one's own agenda.

When the patient has come to terms with his or her fate in the acceptance stage, the family may be more in need of moral support than the patient. It is imperative that families are helped to understand that distancing and emotional withdrawal are a necessity for the dying person. Family members and friends, therefore, should not feel rejected or abandoned by the loved one who is preparing to leave them.

Let us be mindful that the psychological stages a person passes through, until an acceptance of death is reached, are ways of dealing with the underlying fear. They function as buffers when the overwhelming fear of dying cannot be faced directly. Their manifestations vary greatly, but they are merely changes in scenery on the journey to the destination.

Resignation

How sad to think that not all reach an attitude of acceptance and die peacefully! Too often, instead of going through the dynamic process of dealing with shock, denial, anger, looking for a way out, depression that culminates in acceptance and leads to peace, some take the passive route of *resignation*. Resignation is a stagnant state, devoid of the initiative to take care of the unfinished business in one's life: Life events are not being reviewed, repressed anger is not being dealt with, fears are not acknowledged, tears are not being shed, and closure does not occur—neither with the people in one's life, nor with the responsibilities life brought with it. Resignation tends to leave frustration, discontent, even bitterness in its wake.

With our culture's emphasis on being happy at all costs, suffering becomes awkward. All too often, we try to dull the pain of grief and loss, along with their associated "unhappiness." We prefer to numb ourselves or to escape into shallowness in order not to feel its intensity. We can readily do that in many ways: through incessant television watching, Internet surfing, alcohol, drugs (including prescribed tranquilizers); by becoming a workaholic or sports-fanatic; or by living in books and fantasies. Each of these prevents us from being present to life circumstances that demand our attention, being available to loved ones who may need us.

Resignation may also set in when there is seemingly no one—not even a Higher Power—with whom to share these valleys of life and draw strength from the loving encounter. The suffering person can feel totally alone and forsaken while surrounded by people who cannot or will not "gather together" in the spirit of caring understanding.

Dr. Elisabeth Lukas (1986) is a psychotherapist and a foremost proponent of Viktor Frankl's work who challenged her colleagues to dare to stand by in empathy in cases when a cure is no longer possible. In *Meaning in Suffering*, she stated:

Faith in God has been shaken in many people's
lives, and interpersonal support even more so. In
our loneliness, we seek from strangers what we
can no longer find in a firm faith or from people
close to us. Psychotherapists, this "last hope,"
cannot afford to say "here I cannot help, this goes
beyond my field of competence." Where the scientific
knowledge fails, humanity must take over. At the
limits of understanding, empathy must find words
[expression].

To Lukas, therapists who limit themselves to what is
curable practice their profession but fail in their vocation.

As sobering as these statements may be, they also
imply that no other work is better suited to help us face
our own human frailties and mortality. Nothing lends
itself more to tending our own inner growth than being
present to others on their journey though suffering. To
be instrumental in assisting others to prepare for their
transition and to help them find acceptance and peace
has its own rewards.

It should be pointed out that Kübler-Ross's attitudinal
stages are not only encountered in facing the fear of
death, but they are also met during any type of loss we
experience, though perhaps to a lesser degree. We can
go through the same attitudinal reactions in any feared
situation that entails predictable loss and follow the same
processes, actively or passively. If we choose to do all that
we can do when faced with an unchangeable fate or loss,
we will eventually surrender into acceptance and find
peace in spite of our fate—knowing that we have done
our best. If, however, we just resign ourselves without
participating in the process of transformation, we may
reap discontent.

The transformative process—inherent in unavoidable
suffering—makes us realize that tragedy often contains

the seeds of grace: We can become more than we were before, by facing the challenges life presents to us. Thus, our humanness unfolds.

My own process of transitioning through these stages of attitudinal shifts, from shock and attendant denial to decisive acceptance, was very rapid, yet discernible in retrospect. First, there was the *shock* of discovering that I could not move following the excruciating pain I had felt upon impact. This shock reverberated through my entire being. The realization that I was paralyzed and obviously severely injured led to the logical conclusion that I would die—probably very soon. There was little time for *denial*. My greatest fear at that stage was associated with the possibility of being kept alive through artificial means.

Intense *anger* surfaced when the phone kept ringing and I had to confront my helplessness. It would have been in easy reach before, but now I could not lift the receiver or use it in any way to call for help. Given the circumstances, there was little room for *bargaining*. If anything, I wished to die faster rather than to prolong the agony and anguish I was experiencing. There was mounting evidence of my rapidly worsening condition. That brought up the urgency to "put my house in order" as much as was possible in my predicament. *Depression*? There was tremendous sadness that I could not reach out to people I loved dearly to say good-bye, and profound grief that I could not even extend a final greeting and a mother's blessing to my children.

Enter Grace! To what else can I attribute that remarkable adventure inward, but grace? I was guided through a life review that revealed situations from a different perspective than I had viewed them before. It was no longer a matter of judging something "right" or "wrong"; but rather, "was that the 'best' choice in a given circumstance?" And ultimately the question, "What have you learned from the experiences undergone?" By that standard, perceived failures, as well as seeming triumphs, took on different meanings than I had ascribed to them before. This life review led to an *acceptance* of who I had become as a result of having lived. It also brought me to an acceptance of my impending death.

ಬಿ

Perceiving or assessing another's readiness to explore the subject of death with its attendant fears and anxieties is a delicate matter. Assumptions and preconceptions based on church attendance, for example, are out of place here. When one goes to do battle on these intense fronts of life, it is helpful to wear the armor of vulnerability and to look for the possibility of an open window in the other. To care enough to be with someone center to center, or soul to soul, requires courage and sensitivity. Be that someone—or find someone—who will assist your loved one to enter the next dimension with spiritual poise.

This understanding allows us to approach each person as God's unique creation and expression, especially when interacting with those who are preparing to take leave from life as we know it. Thomas Moore (1992) emphasized that the individual must cultivate depth as well as sacredness to engage in soul work. These qualities, I would like to add, should be nurtured by both counselor and counselee, psychotherapist and client, family member or friend and loved one.

Above all, the most desirable skill to cultivate, before attempting to serve others, is the *art of listening*. This is true for the professional and layperson. Some have called it *being present*, others refer to it as *with-ness*. Whatever name we give it matters little. Such active listening embraces a form of spiritual intelligence, which perceives beyond ordinary cognition. It simply knows! It knows how to establish a safe space for dialogue, when dialogue is necessary. It fosters an atmosphere of tranquility and harmony that creates sacred space, where communication beyond words is possible. Above all, listening—the gift of attention—is what we need to practice when assisting others on their journey home.

℃

The child psychiatrist, Dr. Jerry Jampolsky, while working with dying children, found that his young patients had often lost their fear of dying long before their parents could accept the inevitable. In the hope of transforming his patients' and their families' fears, he founded The Center for Attitudinal Healing in Tiburon, California. Ways of transforming fear (particularly the fear of death) into love are taught there and practiced in structured support groups with remarkable success. He describes the principles of attitudinal healing and their transformational process in his book, *Teach only Love.* An example will illustrate the power of communication beyond words, the premise of just being present. An encounter with a gravely ill, hospitalized patient by the name of Mary is told in this manner:

> Of the many things Mary and I taught each other, the most significant was that words are not necessary. The best moments we spent together were the silent ones, with joined hands and in prayer, giving gratitude for being in God's presence and feeling the infinity of His peace and love. As her trust in God increased, her peace radiated, and her family began to feel their fears dissipate.

⵷

It may be the exceptional person who can be present
to another human being in this way, but they do exist!
Fiona Cartmell is a practitioner of aromatherapy and
reflexology at the Royal Edinburgh Psychiatric Hospital
in Scotland; she gave a vivid example:

> I try to practice what Viktor Frankl calls "medical
> ministry" through offering healing touch: by being
> present in a compassionate, non-judgmental way;
> by listening with my heart, mind, and soul—to even
> the most distant, lost whispers of the patients I
> encounter.

> Where elderly patients are concerned... (some are
> even in the last days of life who have already lost
> the ability to communicate with speech that could
> be recognized as coherent) I try, then, in the silence
> of prayer, and with touch, to communicate from my
> soul to their soul. I hope that on some level, this
> enables us to communicate, human being to human
> being.

> Recently, an elderly man who was close to death,
> and was heavily sedated with morphine, gently
> squeezed my hand. In the silence of my prayers
> for his transition, and in my "anointing" of him
> with fragrant oils, I hoped that this tiny movement
> of his hand was a sign that something had been
> communicated.

Such is the power of altruistic love, of self-transcending
caring. It touches the very soul of the other. It also liber-
ates the giver of such love from the fetters of fear. Death
turns into a commonplace matter, and its reign of fear
diminishes. As a consequence, life seems cast upon a
higher plane. Grace has touched the lives of both the giver
and the receiver of such self-transcending love.

෩

These examples point to transformation occurring
when spirit, the inner-living selfhood, is touched in the
familial encounter, friendship, or therapeutic relationship.
Where there is love—active concern for the well-being
and spiritual growth of another—the mysterious working
of Grace as the silent third partner can be anticipated.
When journeying with others in self-transcending love,
we can relate it to the spiritual fire described by Teilhard
de Chardin (1975):

> *The day will come when, after harnessing space,*
> *the winds, the tides, and gravitation, we shall*
> *harness for God the energies of love. And on*
> *that day, for the second time in the history of the*
> *world, we shall have discovered fire.*

4. Help along the Journey

If fear is the greatest impediment to progress,
Peace is its greatest facilitator.
Pope John Paul II

There are some helpful approaches to face our mortality while death is still in the distance. A strong and healthy person, who reflects periodically upon life and death, will be far less frightened by life's approaching end than someone who has not thought about it until death is at the door.

Among the least traumatic and intrusive methods of approaching fear in general, and the fear of death in particular, are imagery techniques which gently lead a person to face fearful situations and circumstances. A veritable cornucopia of such practices, from East and West, can be found. Imagery or visualization can be practiced alone or with a helper. It can be an exercise in letting go of fear and of attachments that hold us back. It can be a form of spontaneous prayer or meditation.

The following universally applicable imagery can be easily adapted to a person's own idiomatic language if need be.

Journey to your Interior Castle

Place yourself in a comfortable position, where your body will be supported and safe for an extended period of time. When you have done that, slowly close your eyes.

Now that you are comfortably settled, we can begin our imaginary journey.

Listen to the following as you would listen to a fairy tale: with a childlike sense of awe and wonder. On this little journey you will go to your interior castle—on an imaginal plane of awareness. In an attitude of relaxed alertness, let your mind drift... the way you do when you day-dream or dream at night. The first thing you will probably notice is a sense of freedom and lightness.

To begin, visualize a path... a path leading through a beautiful meadow full of grasses and flowers, and a soft mountain breeze is blowing. Follow this path into a deep forest where the tall trees look like cathedrals of nature. Here the air is pure and crisp. Inhale deeply this fresh clean air and feel yourself becoming even freer and lighter yet—as you are filled with pure cleansing air and the breeze is blowing through you.

In the distance you can faintly hear the gurgling of a mountain stream. Follow the sound and soon you will come to a stream with its inviting water. Step into the refreshing water and let it wash over you. Bathe in it and wash away any weariness you want to leave behind. Again, experience yourself becoming even lighter, freer, cleaner.

Cleansed by air and washed by water, let us continue the journey. Ahead is a bridge. This bridge leads from tangible reality to the land of Higher Consciousness—a less tangible dimension, but equally real. This bridge is made of light in the colors of the rainbow.

Red. The nearest ray is the red ray. Immerse yourself in its vibrancy and take on those energies from the color red that your physical body may need for vitality. Take on as much of this energy as you want for now and then move on to the next ray.

Orange. Orange is stimulating to our emotional well-being. Like flames dancing in the fireplace, orange gives us the glow of emotional warmth. When you have basked in the orange ray to your heart's content, let's move on to the next ray.

Yellow. Like a ray of sunshine, yellow feels so good; it warms, invigorates, empowers. Let this sunny yellow penetrate all the recesses of your entire being, giving you more aliveness and clarity in decision making. After you have absorbed as much of this yellow light as you need for now, let us move on to the next ray of the rainbow.

Green. You might want to envision the lush green of verdant pastures. Green is soothing. It is peaceful. It is healing and expansive. Immerse yourself in this beautiful green and feel an abundance of well-being spilling into every area of your life. Take on as much of this green ray as you can hold and prepare to leave green with gratitude to traverse the next color.

Blue. Imagine the blue of a cloudless summer sky— blue that inspires, blue that beckons onward and upward. Blue enhances the ability to communicate and express yourself. Drink in this beautiful blue until you feel your spirit lifting higher and higher. The blue of the sky seemingly has no limits, no boundaries. It goes on and on until it deepens into the color indigo, the color of the sky at night.

Indigo. That deep midnight blue, so mysterious... Yet, you sense that anything is possible here. Move through the color indigo now and allow it to assist you in opening to the mysteries inside of you, to get in touch with that part of you that is full of awe and wonder—innately yours, yet often hidden from your conscious awareness. Allow yourself to be in touch with your depth, your heights, while traversing indigo. From indigo it is but one step into the color violet.

Violet. The last visible color in the spectrum of differentiated light is violet. Glide into violet now and experience yourself totally surrounded and filled with the color violet. Let the violet ray blaze through your entire being, transforming all the conditions and situations in your life—internal and external—anything you are aware of that wants to be purified and transmuted before you move on.

We need to leave the heaviness of earthly life behind before we can cross over the threshold to higher consciousness. We want to leave the crude, the base behind us. We have embarked upon a path of transformation into something finer, purer, more sensitive that lies ahead. Crossing the Rainbow Bridge is a way of attuning to subtler energies.

[Some may want to stop here initially:

If so, bask in the golden-white light beyond the rainbow; absorb as much of that healing light as you need by surrounding and filling yourself completely. And, when you are ready to return, slide back down on the rainbow, cross the little mountain stream, take the path through the forest, the meadow that takes you back to where your body is resting. Slowly awaken from this imaginary daydream, feeling refreshed and invigorated.]

ॐ

To continue:

Are you ready to step off the Rainbow Bridge and enter the land of Higher Consciousness? If so, you will find yourself standing before a gate, the gate to the Crystal

City. Here we no longer encounter light as broken down into the color spectrum, but undifferentiated, crystal clear light. The gate opens at your touch. You enter and find yourself on an avenue leading through the Crystal City. Walking down this avenue, you may see wondrous sights:

- Places of healing
- Halls of learning
- Temples of wisdom
- Shrines for worship
- Mansions belonging to your brothers and sisters.

As you walk along, start to look for your own dwelling place. And you come to it at the end of the road—your own interior castle. Doesn't it look familiar? You are the master mason who has crafted this edifice. This is your inner dwelling place.

Walk up the stairs to your very own castle now. You can anticipate finding real treasures here. This is the storehouse of your inner strengths and resources. Your interior castle was built from the unique gifts you were endowed with by your Creator.

Slowly open the door and behold all the treasure that is here! Look upon its magnificence. Acquaint yourself with some of the works of art in here. Do you recognize them? They were crafted by your choices and consequent actions from the raw materials with which you were endowed. These artifacts were chiseled by the life challenges you mastered. These works are representative of the triumphs and seeming defeats in your life—evidence of your learning and growth.

Are you pleased with the reflection of who you are or do you want to initiate changes? If so, you can proceed to the deeper interior of your castle.

At the far end of your interior castle, there is a Holy of Holies. As you approach inward, you can see an altar.

An altar is a place of change, of alteration, of transmutation. Any change we want to have manifested externally begins with change internally—as a change in attitude or vision.

You have come to this altar, into this state of stillness, because you want to transmute or transform something in your consciousness, and you are seeking guidance from your Higher Self. This is a sacred encounter. Your Higher Self is that part of you that personifies the noblest elements of your being. It is that unique individuation of Divinity that finds expression through you.

Your Higher Self is that true inner friend who knows you so well; the one whom you can trust completely; who interacts with you intuitively; who has your highest good at heart. When you attune yourself to its guidance, you are in communion with your Source. You are guided by unconditional love in the direction of your highest good.

In this state of inner stillness, your Holy of Holies, your Higher Self is expecting you. Feel yourself warmly welcomed and joyously greeted. Intuitively you know that this contact is important to help you realize your vocation of destiny. Your Higher Self is there for you always, but you have to be receptive to its guidance in order to change or transform attitudes in yourself.

If it is your fear of death you want to release (or anything else you may wish to change), give it a shape or form, then place it upon this altar of transformation. Allow your Higher Self to help you transmute it into energy that is useful to you, that will help you to accomplish your life tasks.

Ask your Higher Self now, "What do I need to know, to change, to do so I can live a life filled with joy, harmony, meaning, and purpose?"

Your answers may come as visual or auditory impressions, feelings, inspiration, or intuitive knowing. Be still now and await guidance from within.

[Long pause]

After you have communed with your Higher Self, give thanks! Express your gratitude for the guidance you have received and for the encouragement, love, and support that has been given you throughout time.

Know that this help is always available to you—here at the altar of your own interior castle—which is a metaphor for that state of being where you experience the living love inside you!

When you are ready to leave this inner dimension, retrace your steps by symbolically closing the door of your interior castle. Go down the steps leading to the avenue... walk back through the Crystal City until you pass through the gate.

You can return from the land of Higher Consciousness by crossing the Rainbow Bridge and sliding down to Earth on your favorite color of the rainbow. When you have done that, you'll find yourself back on the path, which leads through the forest, the meadow, back to where your body is resting.

Your consciousness is bringing back all that you have experienced in this expanded state of awareness, along with a deep peacefulness and sense of well-being.

Gradually return to your waking state, feeling refreshed, integrated, and alert. Take a deep breath or two... wiggle your fingers and your toes... stretch a little... and slowly open your eyes.

Welcome back!

Postscript. This imagery technique was once practiced during a retreat attended mostly by teens with incurable illnesses. As these young people engaged their imaginations, they felt empowered to experience rich resources within themselves. Instead of feeling totally victimized by their disease, they found a way to co-create their life on an inner dimension of existence.

One young man put it this way: "I felt like I went to some 'wonderful, wonderful Land of Oz' where I could explore things and do things I can't while I am stuck in my aching body."

Another chimed in: "I am going to go back there! Now that I know how to get there; all I have to do is cross the Rainbow Bridge and enter another world. I am not scared any more!"

∞

Through imagery we can approximate and pre-live life situations that are extremely difficult to face any other way—the fear of death, for instance. Once we have taken that initial step toward facing our fears, they begin to dissipate. Only after we come to accept death as part of life, can we live authentically. We can start to live more fully in the present, recognizing that Life is a gift. Then we can respond to the Giver of Life with gratitude and love, instead of fear.

Dr. Kübler-Ross found when working with terminally ill children that they were not afraid of dying, but of being put in the ground and left there. They may have attended a funeral or seen it on TV where someone was put in a box, then lowered into a hole in the ground, and left in the cemetery with dirt shoveled on top. That is very scary to little children.

Engaging the children's imagination to help them change that frame of reference helped greatly to alleviate their fears. Dr. Kübler-Ross used the analogy of the butterfly leaving its cocoon behind and flying free when the cocoon had served its purpose. By explaining that it is only the cocoon that is buried, long after the butterfly has flown away, there was nothing to fear. She further emphasized that the place of burial, the cemetery, is for those who are left behind. They can come there to pay their respects, perhaps bring flowers, and lovingly remember the person who has gone on.

Is it not comforting, even exciting, to imagine that at the moment of death we are able to leave behind the cocoon of a worn-out body and fly free—like a butterfly—to explore other dimensions of existence?

Mystery of Life Discussion

The Brazilian psychiatrist, Dr. Roberto Rodrigues, described to me an approach he has found to be very successful with his patients, which he terms *the Mystery of Life Discussion.* He cautions that there are no fixed techniques to deal with the mystery of life. It is improvisational, yet very genuine. The only guideline is to preserve respect and existential presence in the therapeutic relationship with a suffering person. Then the catharsis, openness, and search for meaning and authentic values can be realized. Dr. Rodrigues presented the idea for this dialogue to his patients in this simple manner:

> Together we will read the book of your life. This book is personal and there are no equals to it in the whole world. It's up to you to find meaning in it and to write some other fascinating chapters. I'll be here to help, but you were, are, and will be the author of the book, *The Mystery of my Life.* Let's begin!

The introduction of such a dialogue can be very valuable. It facilitates a life review; it finds meaningful goals yet to be fulfilled; it looks for areas in life where completions are needed. The mystery of life dialogue can be expanded to include psycho-spiritual issues, such as the fear of death. The efficacy of such a dialogue lies in the naturalness of it.

Such a life review can be extended into a life preview, culminating on the last day of one's life. Then the overarching question becomes, "What will I need to have done, or what kind of person will I need to have been, in order to feel fulfilled on the last day of my life?" This encourages one to ponder: What will I leave behind that will be of value to others? What significant tasks have I accomplished? What remains to be done? Are my relationships with others harmonious? If not, how can I bring about reconciliation or extend forgiveness? Answers to such questions will determine the legacy I leave behind—how I will be remembered.

For those who are courageous, envisioning the inscription on their tombstone or listening to the eulogies being delivered at their memorial service—in their imaginations, of course—might prove insightful.

Death ceases to be so frightening when one chooses to become acquainted with the "foe." Taking that step inevitably leads to examining the life one is living and making course corrections, if necessary. For some, death then becomes the next great adventure, an experience to be eagerly anticipated when life draws to its natural conclusion, not an event to be dreaded and feared.

The Impact of Story

I once knew a brave grandmother who drew great strength from her faith in God and the teachings of her religion in an afterlife. She could calmly accept her impending death and wanted to find a memorable way to prepare her young grandchildren for her departure without inducing emotional distance or instilling fear. It had to be very simple because some of them, as she put it, were "iddy-biddy." After considering several scenarios, she presented her leaving to them in the following way:

> My little darlings, as you know, grandma likes to go on trips. She likes to go to far-away places, to experience new and exciting things. Well, grandma is getting ready to go on a long, long trip. Only this time she is not coming back. She is going to stay in that faraway land. Even though you won't see her, she will be with you whenever you think of her and remember her. Grandma loves you very much. Her love will stay with you always.

> Soon it will be time for her to make this l-o-n-g journey. Grandma has been preparing for this trip all her life. This is one trip we all have to make one day.

> A long, long time from now, when it will be your turn to make that journey, just know that grandma is already there. If she could make it to that faraway land, so can you!

This high-spirited grandmother made a game of her recital. Every weekend when her young grandchildren came to visit, she would repeat her story and then ask them, "Where is grandma going?"

The chorus of little voices would answer, "On a l-o-n-g trip—to a land far, far away."

"When is grandma coming back?" she would ask.

"Grandma isn't coming back," they would reply.

"Why not?" she wanted to know.

"Because it's too far away; but we'll go there too some day," the children would answer.

"Even you?" she'd inquire of each one.

"Yes, even I! But not for a long, long while yet," a young voice would reply.

"Are you going to be afraid to make that long, long journey some day?" Grandma wanted to know.

"NO!" would be the resounding response, "Because grandma is already there!"

Although they had only about six weeks to rehearse their recital, I am sure it will have a lifelong impact on the hearts and minds of her dearly beloved grandchildren. She died knowing that she had accomplished a very meaningful last task she had set for herself. She not only demonstrated a peaceful transition to all who knew her, but she was also able to plant seeds in young minds and hearts that death need not be feared.

The Arts as Vehicles for Transformation

Since ancient times, death has inspired literature, the visual arts, and music. The Greek tragedies, works by Dante, Goethe, Shakespeare, Rumi, Blake, Tolstoy, and other literary giants attest to it. Michelangelo purportedly said, while carving his Pietà, "No thought exists in me which death has not carved with his chisel." Burial pyramids, monuments in stone, bas-reliefs, and innumerable paintings on walls and canvas depict scenes associated with death, resurrection, and ascension—speculating about an afterlife and the soul's journey onward.

For some who are facing their fear of dying, art—in its myriad forms of expression—may be the medium that will lead to acceptance of fate and bring inner peace. The following example will serve to illustrate the importance of art as a therapeutic vehicle.

The Case of Father Joseph

During a professional seminar I was approached by a colleague who was seeking help for one of his clients, a Catholic priest who had suffered a heart attack. Although he was making a good recovery medically, he was despondent, going through the motions of living without being alive. His community was concerned and sought help for his psychological malaise. My colleague had tried numerous interventions to no avail. Discouraged, he asked me if I would see his client. He hoped that my area of expertise, Viktor Frankl's logotherapy, might make a difference.

When I met "Father Joseph," (not his real name) my first impression was: Here is a noble soul, caught in an existential vacuum or inner emptiness. He seemed at ease and readily told me how he began his religious formation at the pre-seminary level, at age fourteen. He liked the high ideals that his religious order espoused. He entered the religious life as a very young man and, in time, became a priest. For more than four decades he performed the duties assigned to him faithfully and unquestioningly. Then his heart stopped. Since his heart attack, he had been reviewing his life, questioning the value of some of the rules he had lived by and fearing he would have another heart attack.

I asked him if having another heart attack was his greatest fear. He answered, "No, not the heart attack per se. But, if that were the end, I'd stand there before God with my *emptiness*, with no return on the talents He had entrusted to me."

When I tried to point out his long years of faithful service as a priest, he brushed it aside, saying firmly, "I did my duty!" Then I asked him what specific talent he felt he was given by God that could yet be increased.

A smile spread slowly across his face. Shyly he said, "Sometimes I fancied myself a painter. ...Oh, I've had art classes here and there, but there has never been enough time to devote to painting."

I suggested that perhaps now, while he was convalescing, there could be time for painting. He nodded thoughtfully, saying, "Yes, I could take my easel and move into our hermitage for a while and just paint. Yes—I'd like that!"

At last, I detected a spark of aliveness returning with the anticipation of a personally meaningful creative endeavor ahead. Spiritual vitality was being activated. Here was something freely chosen that he wanted to do, something that was not subject to compliance with extrinsic rules, but had intrinsic value for him.

For several months Father Joseph painted. Off and on, when he was in town, he came to see me. A transformative change was observable in him. One day, he described his experience while painting: "You know, as a member of a religious order, prayer has played an important role in my life. I've prayed for people, I've prayed with people. Prayer has been my way of communicating with God and interceding for others. But this is different! When I'm totally immersed in painting, it's beyond communicating. It's like being in total communion with my Creator and His entire creation. Ah, if this is what heaven is like, I'm ready."

I thought I heard a longing in his voice to stay in that expanded state of being in communion with God. The week after this conversation took place, Father Joseph died of a massive heart attack. He died at peace. The transformation of his attitude—from fearing to stand before his Creator in his emptiness, to joyous anticipation of being in total communion with Him—was made possible through immersion in the art of painting. For Father Joseph, painting helped to facilitate the numinous experience of union with the sacred.

The Power of Music

Some musicologists believe that the earliest music probably consisted of lamentations and funeral dirges. Among classical composers, death is the motif that inspired music by such masters as Bach, Handel, Hayden, Mozart, Beethoven, Brahms, Bruckner, Wagner, Schubert, Liszt, Mahler, and many others. The power of music is well known. In particular, sacred music that is meaningful to the listener can be a rich source of inspiration and solace. We can feel its power when singing hymns and spirituals.

A young mother related her tremendously uplifting experience with music:

> After weeks of caring for our gravely ill child, my husband urged me one evening to go to the symphony while he took over at our son's bedside. Although I felt guilty leaving them alone, it turned out to be the best thing I could have done.
>
> I had always resonated to the music of Beethoven. That evening, I experienced his Ninth Symphony as never before. The chorus carried me to the Elysium whereof they sang. I experienced something sublime. I felt renewed in every way—ready to return to take my place at the bedside of our critically ill child again.

Many of us find that sublime music, which helps our spirits soar, can usher us into experiencing expanded consciousness. Those of us who love to explore new frontiers could use this method to voyage into realms beyond the finite limits of waking consciousness. Once we have a foretaste of the wider places that await us, the fear associated with "the end" vanishes. Death becomes the doorway to that greater reality after each has fulfilled life's purpose and is ready to leave the mortal phase of existence behind.

Musical tastes, as well as individual tastes in all the arts, vary greatly and we all have our preferences. One of my personal favorites for expressing the return of a soul to its place of origin is the inspired music by the same title as this book, *The Journey Home*, composed and performed by Micah R. Sadigh (see A-V Resources in the bibliography).

ɞ

Reflection

In light of my own adventure inward, I reflected on the diverse approaches people have found to help themselves and others rise above their fears. It reinforced my conviction that numinous or profoundly intuitive experiences are our common birthright. As human beings on the path of ascending toward greater wisdom and spiritual awareness, we are destined to have these inner experiences that are life changing. In their wake, it is only natural to want to share these treasured insights with others in order to uplift and be of help along the journey.

5. Journeying in Faith

Faith is an oasis
the caravan of reason will never reach.
Kahlil Gibran

We all have our cherished beliefs, especially in things born of promise. When this belief is tested and strengthened, it becomes faith. Such faith or inner conviction that is acquired through personal experience will become truth manifest in a person's life. This kind of *experiential knowing* is real, no longer hearsay.

Such was the case for me when my belief in the continuation of consciousness or survival beyond death was confirmed by direct experience. What is experience? We could look at it as the interplay between expectant imagination and external reality. When they converge, then that which was only imagined becomes real, and we are left with an experiential truth that is ours to have and to hold. Now that I *know* that life continues after death, it is no longer a matter of imagined belief only, but a truth I cherish and a faith I trust.

Many faith traditions admonish their adherents to believe in an afterlife, and many of their faithful so believe. This is a wonderful first step in the development of faith. However, such teachings become our truth through directly perceived inner knowing.

Pramahansa Yogananda, the first great master from the East who came to live and teach in the West, received this invaluable advice from his guru before leaving India:

> Exchange unprofitable speculation for actual God-communion... Clear your mind of dogmatic theological debris; let in the fresh, healing waters of direct perception.

> Attune yourself to the active inner Guidance. He only is wise who devotes himself to realizing, not reading only, the ancient revelations.

And how was this "God-communion" to be accomplished? By cultivating "spiritual awe," Yogananda was told. This is the attitude that predisposes us to be receptive to the inflow of inner knowing.

In Judeo-Christian, Islamic, and other faith traditions we have many examples of spiritual awe that led to direct perception of something great and glorious. The attitude of wonderment, of being in a state of deep inner silence, fosters receptivity for higher wisdom and inspiration. There is hardly a better time for such awe-filled contemplation regarding one's relationship to that mystery we call God than when contemplating one's own death. Some will be conscious of a deep experience when entering into such mysterious communication; all will be blessed, even though they might not be conscious of it.

The Catholic scholar, Ewert Cousins, in his visionary book, *Christ of the 21st Century*, describes this enlarged perception which leads to deeply meaningful experiences and sacred encounters:

> I use the term "mystery of Christ" for this ground that was experienced on a deep spiritual level— beyond that of doctrinal formulations. It was a mystery not merely in the sense that it could not

be formulated adequately in abstract rational categories, but primarily in the sense that its reality was so vast and profound that it could never be fully drawn into reflexive awareness.

When we enter into God-communion at that profound level of reality, transformation of consciousness occurs. Fears are transmuted. Peace, love, and hope prevail. If the dying person can reach that state of awareness, the preparation for the transition is accomplished.

Regarding the "Hereafter" or an "Afterlife"

Many traditions speak of some kind of existence after death. We encounter portrayals of life beyond death in various religious teachings, folklore, mythology, and fables. Descriptions of the afterlife vary according to time and place, and what is most significant is their persistent recurrence across cultures.

In the annals of sacred writings, Jesus Christ gave humanity the most hopeful and explicit promise of the continuation of life beyond death when he told his apostles that he was returning to the Father that they might have life everlasting. Furthermore, emphasizing the Fatherhood of God and the brotherhood of men, he declared: "I ascend unto my Father, and your Father; and to my God and your God" (John 20:17).

His assurance of "everlasting life" was so revolutionary that few could believe it, then or now. By and large, nearly two thousand years after such a revelation, his followers still primarily focus on his crucifixion instead of his ascension. His salvific message was intended for all members of the human family, not just for those who are called "Christians." As we glimpse the truth of his promise, our vistas expand to embrace an unshakable faith that life continues beyond the portal of death.

ℰℐ

The following is a treasured memoir from my friend Rachel's family history. No doubt, it has greatly influenced successive generations of this family in their belief in the continuation of life beyond the grave, as well as in their vocational choices, as several—including Rachel—have become ministers.

The Last Days of Harry Chester Buck
Marion Stearns Buck

Having been requested to write an account of the last days of my boy Harry, I will try to do so as best I can...

In the Spring of the year 1882, my family, consisting of my husband, myself, and six children, were living in Easton, Massachusetts. My youngest child, a girl not six months old, had passed to the other side in November 1876.

In that spring of 1882 diphtheria attacked us, and on the 16th of May, our oldest boy, Horace, not quite eighteen years of age, was taken from earth. When he realized that he must go, he spoke calmly and pleasantly of it, and said, "It is all right." In one week from that time on the 23rd of the month, my husband followed our boy. On the 29th my second son, Howard, thirteen years old, was with his father and brother. Almost his last words were the Lord's Prayer, as he was accustomed to repeat it before sleeping each night. Then he was gone as quietly as if it was only for a night's rest.

My next child, Harry, eleven years of age, stayed with us until July 8th. The last four days he was with us, he was consciously in both worlds at times. He said he saw his father and brothers as plainly as he saw me.

At another time Harry said to me, "There are four girls with father, and the little one looks like you." I asked, "What is her name?" He replied, "I do not know." Then I said, "Ask your father." He did so, and said, "Father says her name is Evelyn." It was my baby's name. My husband had three sisters who were called to go at an early age, and I thought it might be they who were with him. Harry said the little girl was about as big as George (his brother who was then eight years old). My little girl would have been six if she had stayed with us. In a more congenial sphere they may develop in a shorter time than on the earth.

Harry spoke often of his brother Howard and the little girl being beside him. At one time he told me, "Howard brings me water to drink and it does not hurt me like the water you give me; he knows when I want it without my telling him."

At another time he spoke of the house his father and brothers were in, as a large house, as he expressed it, "five times bigger than this one, and I went up a good many stairs to get to the room they were in." As he was very fond of flowers, I asked if he saw any. He answered, "Not in the room they were in, but in the rooms I went through to get there I saw some." "What kind were they?" I asked. He replied, "They were kinds I had never seen before."

Once he said, "There is a black-haired man with father." I asked, "Who is it?" His answer was, "I do not know." By the description he gave, I thought it might be an uncle of his father's, one he was much attached to, who had gone from earth some years before Harry was born. I had a small picture of this uncle and brought it to Harry. Before I could say a word, he said, "Don't tell me who it is." He took it, looked at it for a moment, then exclaimed, "Uncle Howard... that is the man with father."

He sometimes spoke of other people talking with his father. It seemed to me that my husband was meeting and being welcomed by friends who had gone before. It was a pleasant thought and almost forbade us to mourn for those who still live, and in the Lord's good time we shall meet again.

One day Harry said, "I told him I would come, and I am going." As he spoke he raised himself in bed as if to go. I said, "You will stay with me a little longer, won't you?" He quietly lay down again, but not long after, he went, never to return.

Harry had spoken of his little sister (or the little girl, as he called her) sitting in her father's lap as his father sang to her or told her stories. To me it appeared that my dear husband was with his children and the friends who were with him, and although we were left without his visible presence, yet we should rejoice that they were "all right" as my oldest son had said when he knew that he must go.

Postscript: The fear of diphtheria was so great at that time that Rachel's great-great-grandmother had to read all the funeral services herself at the grave site for her husband and children.

The eight-year-old mentioned in this account, George Buck, also contracted diphtheria, but he survived. He is Rachel's great-grandfather. Rachel's father, Ernest Martin, published this story in *Chrysalis Reader* in 2007.

The explicit intention of this discussion on journeying in faith is to help lessen the fear of death and all it portends. Beyond stating my personal convictions—born of experience and observation—other accounts of similar experiences are included. I leave it to the reader to take what rings true and to leave the rest. It is my fervent hope, however, that such reflections will serve as an incentive to give death and the afterlife some thought. Furthermore, may the outcome of such reflections become the motivation to live life in accordance with one's highest values and noblest truths.

Reflecting on the teachings of revelators of the major world religions, and considering the anecdotal accounts of sincere and valiant people, it emerges that physical death is not the end of life, but a transition to another dimension of awareness on the continuum of life. The preceding anecdote about the impressions of Harry Chester Buck depicted the immediate stage—following mortal life—in the afterlife. It gives the assurance that there is nothing to fear. Life continues much as it was lived while in earthly existence—yet elevated. The emotional ties with family and friends are still intact, which was very comforting to this bereft widow. This brave woman could even rejoice that they were "all right" in spite of her loss of their visible presence.

During this immediate stage following the discarding of the physical shell, personal ties are still strong. This can be viewed as an interim phase on the soul's journey onward. Gradually we will need to leave our three-dimensional trance of earth-side thinking and attachments behind. The progression onward will be into ever-widening spheres of understanding, compassionate inclusion, and love of all creation.

Adjusting to multidimensional realities will be quite an experience! Vast fields of mind are yet to be traversed before the soul can enter the more celestial realms of heaven. There is much learning to be gained in these realms of creative possibilities. The following example, sent by a friend, might be viewed as belonging to a more instructive phase—beyond the immediate stage after death.

A Powerful Dream

Jane Roper

When I was 23 years old, at the end of the turbulent 1960s, my father died after his third heart attack. I was very sad about this as he and I had much unfinished business. Sadly, I realized that I would have to wait a very long time until I saw him again. We would have to resolve those long-standing issues at the far distant time when I too would cross over to the other side of my eternal career. This left me quite unsettled and, as I said, sorrowful.

Several months later, I had a wonderful dream about my Dad. This dream has continued to ease my mind about what he is experiencing, and what I will eventually experience. I would like to share my great dream with you:

I was standing in the dining room of my childhood home and looked out the front window. There was Dad, puttering at the white picket fence that he had built, kneeling on the ground planting geraniums or some such flowers. He loved flowers and even had built a greenhouse in our backyard to enhance his hobby.

When I saw him, I rushed outside—knowing even in the dream that he was dead, but thinking that maybe I could still talk to him. As I approached him,

I started calling out, even before I reached him, so he
wouldn't disappear before I got to him, "Dad, Dad,
tell me, what is heaven like? Do you like it? Tell me
everything about it!"

He looked at me kindly and said, "Well, Janie, I
haven't been here very long, but the best I can tell
right now, it is like a huge university. I am taking
classes, as if I were going to school—taking religion
classes at the University of Michigan" [his alma
mater].

That was a very satisfying answer for me. As I
grew older and continued to search for truth about
the afterlife, more and more I have come to the
conclusion that my dream was quite accurate;
that the entire universe and the eternal ascension
career is, for all of us, to be likened to one great big
school. This realization has given me confidence and
assurance about what lies ahead! These conclusions
have been further continued by my studies of *The
Urantia Book*.

Postscript: Although this dream occurred decades
ago, it is as vivid and consoling to me now as it was
then.

What about Heaven and Hell?

After perusing much of the world's religious literature on beliefs about heaven and hell, I found resonance
with the revelations put forth by the eighteenth-century
Swedish scientist and mystic, Emanuel Swedenborg.

Swedenborg tells us that our nature (who we are, our
character) after death will depend on the kind of life we
have lived in the world. He portrays the afterlife as being
made up of countless communities. The newly arriving
soul in the afterlife, after some rest and re-orientation,
will be attracted to others of similar nature or character.

We will gravitate toward the "Country of Spirit" where we belong. Some will choose the company of noble souls, while others will seek ignoble company because they are acutely uncomfortable in communities that do not reflect their own inclinations.

According to Swedenborg and many other sources, it is not a matter of being "condemned" to hell or "raised" into heaven by arbitrary judgement, but the result of our consistent freewill choosing during life. While on Earth, we face many challenges with their inherent opportunities to choose truth over falsehood, good instead of evil, beauty and kindness above ugliness and malice. In the afterlife we reap the harvest of our choices: How we have used our life energies will become apparent as evidence of who we have become!

Drifting toward the nether or lower worlds, the so-called "hells," is not necessarily an indictment of eternal damnation. Even there, we will have the capacity to want more "light" instead of "darkness." The opportunity for spiritual evolution always exists; however, our habitual choices tend to be guided by our "ruling love" (selfishness or selflessness), which inclines us toward one or another direction or state of being.

Conversely, souls who drift heavenward initially, after their arrival in the afterlife, may want to explore other regions. If they become engrossed in self-love, a narcissistic and pride-filled self-aggrandizement, they may descend, instead of ascend, in their progression onward.

It appears that the soul's evolution is ongoing as states or realms of consciousness are traversed and explored. The objective is to reach ever-greater awareness of God and the immensity of creation—on the journey toward a heavenly home.

After the nearer regions to earthly experiences, such as emotional and mindal realms, are left behind, linear human language becomes inadequate to describe the subtler dimensions. Perhaps music and art are better suited to the interpretation of the celestial realms. Another way to explore such realms is to enter into deep stillness, where love expands into inclusiveness and universality, where we love God and all others with our entire being.

Helen Keller, one of the titans in facing her own adversities of being both deaf and blind, did much to change the way disabled people are viewed and treated worldwide. In an interview on the DVD *Shining Soul*, she shared her convictions regarding death:

> I can't understand why anyone should fear death!
> Life here is more cruel than death. Life divides and
> estranges, while death is life eternal. It reunites and
> reconciles.... I believe, that when the eyes within my
> physical eyes should open upon the world to come,
> I shall simply be consciously in the country of my
> heart.

℞

One remarkable experience of a faith journey was shared with me by Betsy Williams, a hospital chaplain:

> One of my first patients I visited was a lady whom
> the nurse had asked me to see because she had
> stopped dialysis; supposedly, she had only a few
> hours to live.

> I walked into her room expecting to see a person
> ravaged by disease and barely breathing. Instead,
> she was sitting up in bed, wore a beautiful white bed
> jacket, and her cheeks were rosy. I introduced myself

and stated that I had come to visit, and to pray with her—if she would like. She greeted me with a warm smile and invited me to sit on the side of the bed. I did, although I was told in "chaplain school" *not to sit on a patient's bed.*

She promptly said, "I am dying," and added, "I have prepared myself." Then she asked, "Would you like to know what I believe heaven is like?"

Astounded, I nodded, "Yes."

She then told me, "I believe heaven is a place where I will see my husband, and I will have all of my earthly accomplishments reviewed to me. I will enjoy reflecting upon what life on earth has meant to me, and what I have meant to life on earth."

To this novice chaplain it was so amazing to learn that she believed her life had meaning on earth, and that she had meant something to life on earth! We talked a little more, and we prayed. Before I left, I asked her to, please, "put in a good word for me." She said she would. She died peacefully two hours later.

In my opinion, this patient had reached the epitome of self-transcendence: Beyond all the fear, anxiety, and sadness, she had found true meaning and purpose in life and in her impending death. She fully anticipated that her life would be explored, experienced, recognized, and, yes, accepted in a higher dimension.

૪૦

Along with ordinary decent people, Victor Hugo also reflected on the continuity of life and eloquently wrote about it in "The Future Life" (1890):

I feel in myself the future life....

I am rising, I know, toward the sky. The sunshine is over my head; the earth gives me its generous sap, but heaven lights me with the reflection of unknown worlds. You say the soul is nothing but the resultant of bodily powers; why, then, is my soul the more luminous when my bodily powers begin to fail?

When I go down to the grave I can say, like so many others, "I have finished my day's work;" but I cannot say, "I have finished my life." My day's work will begin again the next morning. The tomb is not a blind alley; it is a thoroughfare. It closes in the twilight to open with the dawn.

6. At Journey's End

Your life is a monument!
Viktor Frankl

Dr. Viktor Frankl was a sought-after lecturer around the world until his death in 1997 at the age of 92. In his later years, he was particularly popular with older audiences. His listeners could readily identify with him when he said during a 1984 radio broadcast in Austria:

> We, who have seen so much in this turbulent [twentieth] century, have arrived at the evening of life. Soon we will take the harvest of life experiences to the granaries of life. Nothing can remove our deeds, our loves loved, our hardships bravely borne from the world. Such life experiences are safely stored, like a harvest, which is brought into the granary.

He reminded his listeners that the achievements of our life become our monument—attesting to the fact that we have lived and left something memorable behind.

At journey's end, it becomes the duty and the privilege of the remaining loved ones to celebrate the deceased person's life with a fitting memorial. This may be facilitated by recalling the departed person's accomplishments, the difference she or he has made in the lives of others, their triumphs as well as their defeats, or their courageous suffering. Now they are released to go on, but the harvest of a life needs to be celebrated with gratitude.

In spite of grief, there are responsibilities to be carried out and preparations for fitting memorials to be made.

Serving the Needs of the Living in Grief and Loss

Following a death, the needs of the living must be tended. The admonition of the prophet Isaiah, "Comfort ye, comfort ye my people, saith your God," (Isaiah 40:1), is never truer than in grief and loss. Dying always affects others and those closest to the deceased will feel the most pain. This is particularly the case when death is sudden and unexpected. Certainly, the belief that the loved one will wake up to a new life in another realm may bring comfort, but does not take away the pain of loss. Some even add guilt to their deep sorrow in their bereavement. A pastor with many years of experience, Robert Kirven put it this way:

> I have known bereaved Christians, unquestioningly
> certain that their loved one was living in a new
> way after dying, who felt guilty at having so strong
> a sense of loss and grief. It is as though their
> knowledge of ongoing life was supposed to make
> them somehow superior to death, as if grieving were
> a kind of betrayal of their faith. It is not so.

In *A Book about Dying: Preparing for Eternal Life*, Kirven cites a study with a 25-year follow-up on the psychological effects of grieving. The study began in 1942, following a fire in a Boston restaurant and nightclub, the Coconut Grove, where many people perished. Survivors were interviewed by psychologists, with a follow-up years later. The original interviews revealed two general types among the survivors:

- ◆ One group grieved demonstrably, weeping and repeating details of the tragedy several times during the interview.

♦   The other group was noticeably undemonstrative, speaking with relatively calm resignation of the overall tragedy and their personal loss.

Interviews over a period of 25 years showed that people in the undemonstrative group had received psychological or psychiatric treatment much more frequently than members of the demonstrative group. Kirven concludes that these data, together with his own later experience, convinced him that funerary rituals have significant spiritual and psychological values for the bereaved survivors.

ॐ

Most societies have learned that it is healthy to provide meaningful, socially sanctioned outlets for grief. In connection with funeral rituals and grieving, a student from New Guinea comes to mind. Some years ago, while I was an instructor at a small private college, we had a death at the school. The deceased had been a member of the student council and was well known and liked. After the announcement of her death was made, our students were in shock. It seemed inconceivable to these 18- to 22-year-olds that someone their age could die of an illness. One of our foreign students, Hinabaniku, immediately sought me out and urgently wanted to know, "What do I do? How do I show that I care? What is the custom here?"

I asked her, "What would you do if you were at home now and received news that a friend had died?"

As I remember it, Hinabaniku explained haltingly, even with some embarrassment:

When we hear of someone's death, everyone in the village drops whatever they are doing and heads for the home of the deceased. There, we do what you would probably think of as "mass hysteria." We cry with the family, we wail, we express our sorrow, we grieve together. This goes on until everyone is cried out. Maybe all night, maybe three days, it depends. After the worst of the pain has been released through shrieking, wailing, swooning, or whatever, then we start to tell stories about the deceased. Everyone recalls how they knew him or her, what deeds they remember, what was good about that person, and so on. During this time, everybody brings food and drink. We eat, we talk, we cry, we may even laugh hysterically; the drums talk. It ends when everyone has expressed their feelings and calm is restored.

Then we carry the body, on a litter covered with flowers, in procession—as if the person were going on a journey, accompanied by an honor guard—to the burial ground. The remains are buried, but we think of the person as being on a journey, still part of the tribe, but away from home.

The following year, on the anniversary of the death, we assemble at the grave site. We accept that the person has left us. We mark the grave with a stone, committing them to the past. The year of mourning is officially over. Community life resumes without them, but they live on in the stories we tell about them—so their deeds become their legacy in our oral history.

Compared to the catharsis, expression of condolences, and psychological reintegration available through the communal grieving described by Hinabaniku, our culture has not developed ways of dealing with grief, pain, and loss. To Hinabaniku, our customary ways of visitation at a funeral parlor, followed by a memorial service, must have seemed sterile, cosmetically masked, and tending to denial of death, instead of acceptance of it.

Creating Fitting Memorials

It is meaningful and necessary for the bereaved to honor and celebrate the life that was lived. Memorials designed to commemorate the life of a loved one, who is no longer present in physical form, provide an outlet for transcending the loss the bereaved experience. Death does not end the relationship, but forges a new kind of bond. This bond will not be based on physical presence but on the memory of love shared from heart, mind, and soul with the person who has journeyed on.

Through participation in a commemorative event, making an artifact, writing, playing music, preparing food, gardening, or doing something that is meaningful to the grieving person, grief can be expressed. Emotions are allowed to surface and to be acknowledged. Slowly, consolation is experienced through the recognition that the love that was shared lives on, even though the person is physically absent.

Among the ways to express grief are rites and rituals that are either traditional or unique to a given circumstance. These are deeply meaningful and lead to healing from the loss of a loved one. Some customs surrounding death are an ingrained part of established cultures and religions. They are present in our own culture and are very meaningful to members of our society with that cultural or religious heritage; i.e., the Jewish custom of *sitting shivah*, the Irish *wake,* the Catholic *funeral mass* and praying the *Rosary* for the dead, and other rituals and conventions passed on by tradition. They offer solace to the bereaved.

Included here are some additional ways to express grief and to help facilitate the healing process. These ways either originated as spontaneous expressions or were designed for specific situations or circumstances, yet they have the potential for wider application. The following innovative memorials are presented in an effort to assist the bereaved.

A Word about Cremation

A marked shift in societal norms and customs is occurring that is becoming evident even in the way we look at death and treat the dead. In recent years, we have seen a trend away from the traditional viewing of the body in the casket and subsequent burial in a cemetery. More and more people seem to be moving toward cremation as an ecologically preferred way to dispose of the earthly remains of a departed person. In times past, this may have been the rare exception in our culture, but it is definitely on the increase now.

Cost factors, along with other considerations (such as embalming and viewing of the remains, which are repugnant to some), figure prominently when choosing cremation instead of a costly funeral with all the flourishes. I address this issue here because cremation and dignified closure is under discussion in many circles: families, parishes, retirement communities, churches, nursing homes, etc.

It is important to keep in mind, when considering cremation, that it only changes the physical aspect of "being put to rest." The spiritual and emotional aspects need not be compromised by the choice of cremation. The same type of ceremony, religious ritual, or leave-taking is still available. Cremation does not change the inner dynamic of our beliefs about death or an afterlife; it only changes the outer process of dealing with the lifeless remains. Again, I would like to emphasize that cremation is but an extrinsic process of dissolution, which does not change the spiritual reality of the deceased.

In my own family we had two distinctly different examples of "closure with dignity" that point to changing traditions and personal preferences. My mother had prepared for her departure from this world by purchasing a cemetery plot (nearly 20 years before she needed it) and arranged her prepaid funeral with all the fanfare. She wanted the traditional visitation in the funeral home, as well as burial in the cemetery with the attendant ceremonies and rites of her church. She selected her burial clothes and let it be known that she would like to be surrounded by flowers and her favorite sacred music on the occasion. She left this world in a style that reflected the graciousness of her generation and with the imprint of her personal taste. It was deeply meaningful for all of us to carry out her wishes and to honor her memory in this manner.

On the other hand, my dear sister, Kay, stated emphatically, "Don't you dare put my worn out body on display! I do *not* want to be remembered for how I looked in the coffin! I want to be remembered for who I was in life!" She elected to have her remains cremated, followed by a participatory memorial service. The celebration of my sister's life demanded more creative input from family and friends than did the traditional way mother had chosen. Honoring my sister's wishes provided us with an opportunity to be innovative, creatively expressive, and spiritually authentic when commemorating her life. It, too, was deeply meaningful for us, albeit different. Honoring her expressed wishes meant focusing on what had intrinsic value for her and appreciating who she was in life.

Funeral directors are now offering many innovative options and services to assist families through the difficult decision making and personalization required in the final farewell.

Lastly, a clergy friend, who is often asked whether cremation is an acceptable alternative to the traditional funeral, urged me to address the acceptability of cremation. He further emphasized that, from a psychological perspective, true closure is not really possible until a resting place for the ashes is found following cremation. He graphically pointed out that bringing your spouse, your grandparent, or your infant home in an urn and placing it on the dining room table does not and cannot bring closure to those who grieve. It can readily be seen that this would exacerbate and prolong grief, instead of ameliorating it.

Finding an appropriate way to dispose of the ashes will be another service of love we can render to someone dear. Besides burial or placement of the urn containing the ashes in a cemetery, some have expressed a wish to have their ashes taken to a favorite spot, such as the ocean, a mountain, favorite woods, or family plot.

Just as I was writing about meaningful ways to disperse the ashes of a loved one, a friend called to say that their immediate family was headed north to bury the ashes of his recently departed wife. She wanted to be interred where she was born and had spent her childhood. For her, life had come full circle—from birth to death—and she opted for a symbolically fitting resting place.

Candle Lighting Ceremony

The Center for Attitudinal Healing in Tiburon, California, where death is a frequent occurrence among members of a support group for terminally ill children, has devised a ritual that has been profoundly helpful. If a member of the group has died since the last meeting, the children are told about it. A large candle is placed in the middle of the small circle of children, representing the life of the deceased child. Each of the children is given a smaller candle. They take turns lighting their candle from the center candle and telling how the light of that child lit up their own life. Their loss and grief can be expressed during this ceremony. Death is not denied, but is seen as an integral part of life. The light they have received, from the person who is no longer in their midst, lives on in them and is cherished.

Prenatal Loss Memorial

Since our society would prefer not to discuss pregnancy loss, memorial services for such occasions are largely nonexistent. Yet the pain of the loss is very traumatic for many couples. Penelope Pietras writes about the agony of "Healing from Prenatal Loss." She tells how deeply grateful she and her husband are to the pastor of their church for being willing to create and perform a memorial rite for a stillborn child. This rite helped them to find release from their trauma.

Later, they were instrumental in creating a prenatal loss memorial with others who had suffered similar losses. Penelope states, "A few months ago, in a Denver cemetery, a garden bench was placed on a plot of land that will never hold graves. It is dedicated 'to all those babies who were taken home in their parents' hearts but not in their arms.'"

The idea for such a memorial grew out of their sharing how the acknowledgment of their loss had been a healing event. The idea found ready acceptance among their support group of bereaved parents and became a reality with the help of a hospital chaplain.

Children's Drawings Carried by Balloons

When the need arose to actively include children's participation in a memorial service, The Rev. P. J. Ferris devised a way for young children to express their feelings for a parent or grandparent who had died. The children are encouraged to draw pictures for the person who has left their lives. These pictures express their feelings far better than words. The children's pictures are then attached to helium balloons.

Following the celebration of life service, the children walk up a hill and release their balloons. They watch their pictures rise up into the heavens, taking their greetings and messages to the departed. The tactile activity of drawing, walking, and releasing the balloons is a good way to involve young children in a memorial that is meaningful and memorable to them.

Dealing with Tragic and Sudden Loss

Nikki Peterson related the following occurrence:

In a tragic accident, a 20-year-old driver was killed in the wee hours of a Sunday morning when he lost control of his car and crashed into our house. Although there was considerable damage to the house, fortunately, we and our three young children were not injured. Needless to say, the disaster shattered his family and friends. He was an only child and a well-liked young man.

In the wake of this fatal accident, we witnessed the most amazing outpouring of grief and respect. Hundreds of his young friends came by and mourned him at the site where he had died. They were the sweetest and most respectful kids I've ever met. They kept telling me how sorry they were for what

happened to our home and offered to help clean up
the rubble.

He seemed special to many. All day long his family
and friends kept coming—staring in disbelief at his
car stuck in our home. Their grief was intense as
they held on to each other and cried. As evening fell
that fateful Sunday, about 150 teens gathered on our
lawn to say goodbye to Shay. Setting out flowers and
candles they held a silent candle light vigil for their
friend. It was amazing to experience total silence
from that many kids! Silently and reverently they
paid their last respects to their young friend. We
hope and pray that their spontaneous expressions
of grief and their moving commemoration of him
brought consolation and healing in its wake.

Such spontaneous outpourings of grief in sudden and
unanticipated death offer an outlet for grief that is very
genuine.

Commemoration and Appreciation of Body Donation

Once a year, St. Louis University Medical School
holds a memorial service for those who have donated
their bodies for the purpose of helping medical students
in their training. Families of the donors are invited to
this service, which honors the deceased and comforts the
living by acknowledging that the gift is deeply appreciated.
David Rienstra, whose wife was such a donor, expresses
the intent of the service and the comfort he received from
it in an article titled, "Life's Blessings." He quotes Marin
Martin, a medical student from the class of 2000:

When I think about the kind of person who would
donate her body to this process, I am overwhelmed
by the power of the human spirit. I feel that such a

person embodies the kind of humanity we all aspire to. I would like to personally thank the woman who has and will continue to have such a powerful impact on me...

I am tremendously honored by this gift...with it comes great responsibility. By accepting this gift, I am accepting your trust in me, that your life's effort will be continued in mine... [I will] work my hardest to become the best doctor I can be...

We owe a great debt to the donors. I know the people we are remembering today are sorely missed... I wish I could have met the woman who has become my teacher. I will spend the rest of my life trying to live up to the selfless honor she has shown me.

This moving tribute makes us aware of the grace inherent in gratitude. It was heartwarming to hear not only that the gift was acknowledged, but also that it was received in the spirit in which it was given.

Musical Tributes

In a large metropolitan area, I once witnessed a moving tribute being paid to a long-time member of a men's choir. The all-male choir assembled in the rear of the visitation parlor, taking up their accustomed positions. They sang powerfully and beautifully in unison, offering a musical tribute to their departed "choir brother."

After their last song faded away, they paid their respects individually to the deceased. As the long column of men filed past the coffin, their differences became apparent: Some were young, others old; most were in their middle years. Every size and shape, every racial type and color hue of humanity was represented in this group. Their goodbye gestures were equally diverse, but uniformly respectful. Some wiped a tear from their eyes, while others bowed courteously. Some made the sign of the cross, others offered a salute. There were a few who furtively touched the hand of the deceased in a farewell gesture, while many moved their lips in prayer or whispered a good-bye.

If love of singing brought this group of men together initially, on this occasion they were also united in spirit. They paid their last respects with their gift of song, which only they could offer. It was a most fitting tribute and a deeply moving experience for all who witnessed such unity amidst the diversity of men paying their last respects to a "brother."

Photographic, Audio-Visual, and Internet Memoirs

Inviting the family to make collages with photographs and mementos of the departed family member is another method to involve the bereaved in expressing their feelings through action. Such items are usually readily available. Sifting and sorting through photographs, news clippings, merit badges, certificates, and other memorabilia of the deceased becomes an interactive way of sharing memories, while honoring the family member who has departed. The past comes alive and stronger bonds are created. This is especially important when the fabric of family ties has been rent. Such collages can be prominently displayed during visitation or memorial services. They become keepsakes and serve as photographic memoirs during family gatherings.

Some have assembled such mementos into a book, depicting the departed loved one's life and times. Beginning with the birth certificate and ending with the death certificate, the in-between pages feature highlights from the person's life. It preserves the identity of the deceased in a very personal way. Such books can be readily paged through whenever the occasion warrants reflecting on the past that was shared.

In recent years, the technologically gifted have taken to presenting videos and slide shows of the departed person's life. Posted on the Internet, these can be viewed anywhere by those who are separated by distance and saved for future viewing as well.

Participatory Eulogies

The value of the participatory eulogy cannot be underestimated. In a less formal memorial service, the participatory eulogy serves as a forum for those family members, or anyone close to the deceased, who has something meaningful to share about the departed. Careful selection of participants and time constrains may need to be considered. One way I have seen it done is to suggest a one-page remembrance. Another way to set a time limit is to light a small candle as each participant rises to deliver a portion of the eulogy. It indicates the passage of time and serves as a reminder to the person delivering their part of the eulogy to say what they have to say before the candle goes out.

Often these participants in the eulogy will have known the person being commemorated far better than the minister or someone in that officiating capacity. A greater appreciation for the multifaceted aspects of the loved one, as rendered by different people, often results. These testimonials are very touching tributes, rich in experiential fiber. If at all possible, this format of personal sharing should be encouraged in public commemorations. Participatory eulogies serve as a deeply human way to say, "You have touched my life in a particular way. I will always remember you!"

The Balm of Food

Would any social event, even a memorial service, be complete without food? Food not only nourishes the body; on special occasions, it can be a balm for the soul.

Following a recent memorial service, better named a Celebration of Life Service, we experienced a most fitting contribution to the occasion. It was brought about by the thoughtful blend of heart, head, and hands. The deceased, an older lady, had been renowned for her baking. Rumor had it that Grandma had elevated baking to the ranks of a fine art. It was openly discussed that her artistry would now be a "lost art" in this family circle.

To everyone's joy and delight, a young member of the family had made the effort to re-create one of Grandma's prized recipes. After the funeral, she treated us to one of her legendary desserts. It was such a welcome surprise! It opened the doors to reminiscing about other times when this delicacy had been served by the deceased in bygone years.

This thoughtful remembrance and celebration of the departed family member through this heirloom pastry—made in *her* honor this time—emphasized the bond between family members, as well as ties to their cultural heritage. Realizing that this fine pastry tradition will live on, because the know-how had been passed on to the younger generation, was deeply meaningful. Some even thought that Grandma was smiling in approval!

Memorial Plantings & Gardens

Planting a tree, flowering bush, shrub, or a few flowers is perhaps among the most time-honored ways to create a living memorial. It is ultimately very healing because it requires ongoing care and involvement. Unlike a monument in stone, which once created stands complete, a plant or a garden will need to be carefully tended in times to come. It will stand as a witness to the love that inspired it, brought it forth, and is tending it.

The planted memorial will be deeply meaningful to those who love nature and enjoy watching the seasonally changing cycles of life. It will not only grow and bloom in celebration and commemoration of someone, but will also serve as a powerful symbol of the continuity and regeneration of life. It will bring joy and stand as a gift of hope from the Giver of Life.

ᏸ

The foregoing commemorations of lives, which had arrived at the end of their mortal journey, left me with the indelible impression that the death of someone is a communal event, bar none.

A life completed needs to be acknowledged, remembered, and celebrated with a meaningful tribute. By doing so, those who have departed this life are given the assurance that their lives had meaning, that they accomplished their purpose of touching the lives of others, and are released to journey homeward.

The departed individuals may have crafted the monuments of their lives. However, such monuments need to be set in place by those whose lives were touched by them. Only then can those who remain here be free to transform their grief into gratitude for the love that was shared.

Synopsis

In our rapidly changing world of cultural diversity, religious pluralism, and globalization, one has to be sensitive to individual preferences—especially when

accompanying someone on his or her journey of transition
from this life to the next dimension of existence. Let us
keep in mind that:

 ◆   It takes humility, especially on the part of the
     religious or other professional, to accept *divine
     guidance* when it appears in an unconventional
     guise.

 ◆   It takes discernment to see the *grace of God*
     working in ways that are foreign to our episte-
     mology or belief system.

 ◆   It takes courage to see the *divine essence* in a
     deteriorating physical form, and to be able to
     respond to the greeting of *Namaste* (the Divinity
     in me salutes the Divinity in you) with conviction.

These challenges face us when people, whose religious
and cultural backgrounds are not identical with our own,
come seeking solace.

As more and more people develop greater global
awareness through better communication, travel, and
geographic displacement, they may find themselves
looking for the Universal God in a particular church or
institutional setting.

We cannot continue in our parochial or provincial
attitudes if we want to be able to relate meaningfully
to the needs of suffering human beings in the third
millennium. A convergence of wisdom traditions and
secular spirituality is occurring. A *universal spirituality*
is emerging that will demand open-minded, inclusive,
and creative responses from those who are endeavoring
to serve others. This is particularly true when people
come to us who are facing serious crises in their lives,
such as dealing with death and dying.

∞

An example of one person's preparation for the journey home follows in *Kay's Legacy*. As I look back on the events that preceded and followed her transition, it appears that Kay modeled a consciousness that incorporated many of the characteristics Teilhard de Chardin saw as belonging to *pilgrims of the future.*

7. Kay's Legacy

When she shall die,
Take and cut her into little stars
And she shall make
The face of heaven so bright
That all the world
Will be in Love with night
And pay no worship
To the garish sun.

William Shakespeare

Kay's Insight and Awareness

Kay was not your conventional churchgoer. Having lived in different cultures with varied religious expressions, she had absorbed from them what she found meaningful and spiritually enriching. Added to that was her keen interest in a spirituality that was experiential, not abstract. She was her own person. She knew herself well and understood her role in the scheme of things.

We met one day for one of our talks and she told me about a remarkable experience she recently had while attending a funeral. When the words "dust to dust" were spoken, she heard them as "Light thou art and to Light thou shalt return." This seemed perfectly natural to her. Her next adventure would be into Light!

She also disclosed that she was having a recurrence of a malignancy she had been battling successfully for many years. This time, she felt, she did not have the will, nor the stamina, to combat it. Instead, she would use her remaining time and energy to put her inner house in order and prepare for the journey home. It was very important to her that someone could understand what she was about to undergo, who would be willing to support her spiritual preparation for her *transition into Light*. So it was that I became that someone, among others.

The Helper's Challenge

What happens to us when someone comes with the earnest request, "Please help me prepare myself to die"? As professionals, we have parameters within which we function. The boundaries may be set by doctrinal or professional guidelines. Our toolkit may contain treatment techniques, rites of passage rituals, and traditional prayer formulations. These may serve very well within the convention of which they are an integral part.

But what do we have to offer when we encounter the Kays of this world, who seem to have acquired a universally inclusive spirituality? How do we assist people who seek us out to be available to them, *soul to soul,* as they explore inner territory that is unfamiliar or hitherto untraversed?

Their spiritual quest is genuine and passionate. They do not want yesterday's tradition, nor our rote responses to their needs. Their own process is so dynamic that entering their paradigm, which is existentially relevant to them, becomes the most authentic way to proceed.

So it was with Kay. Since I was both her sister and confidant, who shared in her preparation for impending death, it became the most intense experience imaginable. It challenged our preconceived notions and forced me and others to look for spiritual vitality wherever it could be found.

Her awareness stripped us of pretense and self-righteousness. It demanded an authentic response. In being present to her, life presented us with an opportunity to humbly offer the noblest that was ours to give. Her process was awesome in its grandeur and profound in its depth.

The helpers' contributions consisted primarily in accompanying her on the journey, affirming her in her courageous quest, and supporting and encouraging her exploration of that wider reality she would soon call home. In the end, assisting Kay on her journey into Light was a transforming, expansive, and liberating experience— certainly for Kay, but also for those of us whose lives she touched in the process.

Kay's Example of Conscious Preparation for the Journey Home

Kay began her process of conscious preparation for her transition by systematically withdrawing from her attachments. First she relinquished her business and her clients. Next, she put her belongings in storage and gave up her apartment. She then went into seclusion to sort out her life. Kay spent the next three months evaluating what was essential, what was not, and what needed completion.

She anticipated her good-byes and actively prepared for them. As her energy waned, she became highly selective in how she expended it. She chose more and more the company of a few spiritually attuned friends over the many acquaintances who had made up a large part of her life previously.

This systematic divesting of attachments and leave-taking was a painful process for her. She had enjoyed her career and had many interests and close associations with people. Most painful of all was the final farewell with her grown children.

Healing relationships became her priority because she wanted to leave this world with a clear conscience. She extended forgiveness to those who had hurt her, she expressed gratitude to those who had enriched her life, and she left goodwill and upliftment in her wake. Thus she completed "the monument of her life" with care and forethought.

Beyond that, she left behind a gift: a model for dying that is fearless, adventurous, and joyous—in spite of pain. Kay's gift challenges us to do likewise!

ॐ

During our talks, I quickly discerned that what Kay was looking for in the people she chose as her support network was a certain soul quality.

She wanted very much to do some "healing" of deep wounds she had sustained in life. Initially she was hopeful that if she succeeded to bring closure with forgiveness to some issues in her life, that her physical symptoms, which were manifesting as a recurring malignancy, would go into remission—as they had in the past. To that end, she sought out helpers in various disciplines who, she felt, were kindred spirits.

Lent was approaching, and she believed that Lent would be a good season for spiritual housecleaning. Her fasting for forty days would be primarily a mental fast: a self-imposed discipline of giving up unwholesome thinking and giving up indulgence in emotional negativity.

Her daily diet would include spiritual nourishment: meditation and prayer, inspirational reading, and soul-stirring music. She wanted to withdraw for a while to an environment that was peaceful and conducive to this pursuit.

Our talks centered on transformation: how others, who were the way-showers to humanity, had accomplished this transformation, and which of their ideologies were applicable in the here and now. She wasn't so much interested in the esoteric philosophies, per se, but in the application of their intrinsic principles.

She predisposed herself to deep inner experiences of inspiration and intuitive guidance through an attitude of openness and receptivity. As the busyness of her life was replaced by a sabbatical reflectiveness, with spiritual practices built into her days, a pronounced change was observable. A chrysalis-like transformation was occurring. Her attention shifted from the mundane and peripheral to deeper inner regions. She reached a point in her process where she wanted to reach out to spiritual companions to feel less alone. We devised a meaningful way to invite some of her soul friends into participation without needing to give a lengthy explanation or to expose Kay to humiliation in case her intentions were misunderstood.

After prayerful deliberation, Kay drew up a list of twelve people who had crossed her path sometime in her life and who would understand the nature of her request. She wanted a symbol that could serve as a reminder to them. I helped her obtain twelve large votive candles, violet in color, which burn for one week. She wrote a note asking each recipient to light it on Monday of Holy Week and keep it lit until it went out on Easter. Her note read, in part:

*D*ear _____,

I have been creatively working at reconstructing my body and life, thought by thought, prayer by prayer, letting the deep mystery unfold. Much emotional healing, forgiveness, change... has taken place in these five weeks (at this lovely "hermitage" my sister has provided). Loving ministrations assist me daily.

Now I come with a very special request to some of my most valued and beloved friends. It is the Season of Regeneration in nature. We see it all around us! "Transfiguration" in the deepest spiritual sense is the season's celebration!

I ask that you join me in a Holy Vigil of silent adoration of the Flame of the Resurrection. I have a soul request that you join me in asking for total transmutation of all... that needs to be transmuted. I am only Christ-consciousness liberated into wholeness! Allelujah!

Blessings and much Love,

&

Such was the nature and intensity of Kay's seeking. It demanded the utmost from those of us endeavoring to be helpers, professional or otherwise. Professional distancing was not called for here—but authenticity, creativity, vulnerability, and intuitive perception were essential. Kay seemed to appreciate us most as fellow travelers with whom she could explore possible new horizons.

Reflections of a Goddaughter

Kay, my godmother, enriched my life in so many ways...

My favorite time with Kay was in the weeks before she left us. Life seemed to have come full circle. We talked on the phone about many different things, but this time we were both grownups. She explained, and I understood. She was leaving—and needed to prepare herself. She didn't want to take any excess baggage with her and was sifting and sorting through her life, wanting to take only the wisdom gained from life's experiences with her.

There was no fear, no anger, no tension left in her, just patience and a quiet knowing—and waiting in anticipation—till the time was right to go home....

Audrey Schlote

Recollections of a Nephew

I was home from college during spring break and
helped with the caretaking. Mom explained to me
what was going on physically, psychologically, and
spiritually. It was during one of those nights, while
I was there, that Kay asked me to participate in her
eulogy. I was stunned!

At one point Kay started to slip away, but said later
that a powerful angel pushed her back, saying, "It's
not time yet!"

Toward the end, Kay began to recognize people more
by their inner light than by their physical form. Her
unspoken message seemed to be, "There is an ideal—
we all know it deep within our hearts and minds.
Let us be true to it and work together to make it
manifest in our world."

Ken Westermann

Friends' Impressions of Kay's Last Month

From time to time, Kay requested that we (my husband and I) come to visit her, so we became part of her world.

She liked being surrounded with sunlight, breezes, flowers, and music. There always was an abundance of them all. There was a lightness in and around her as well. She was often smiling.

Kay still had a good appetite and eagerly ate the foods I brought for her. Unfortunately, her stomach couldn't hold much.

During my visits we would pray together silently, peacefully. I sensed a presence, light and loving, in her room.

She gave us a candle to burn for a week, asking that we pray for renewed life. That's how we perceived her request. When the candle went out, I sensed our prayers were somehow answered...

Marion Commerford and John Commerford

Final Farewell

The family assembled Easter Sunday to bid their final farewell. It was a very tearful day. As evening fell, Kay lay totally exhausted upon her bed. She had waited and prepared for this. She had ordered her family affairs to the best of her ability. She had said her good-byes. This was the last important task she wanted to carry out. Now it was accomplished!

The physical renewal she had initially hoped for had not occurred. But a remarkable transformation was going on, especially during the week following Easter, the last week of her life.

She put aside all pain medication, ate hardly anything, became more gentle and inner directed. A deep peace exuded from her. An expectancy of something wonderful beyond words—about to happen—filled her being.

She waited...

Late Sunday evening, one week after Easter, people unexpectedly kept arriving—most of them recipients of her candle.

In the End

She acknowledged our arrival by opening her eyes, looking at us with gratitude. Candles glowed around the room; flowers added fragrance; a gentle breeze was blowing through the open windows; curtains fluttered; chant-like music played softly in the background.

We prayed, sending our light and love to her. We touched her, hoping to convey our love, giving her courage and strength. We formed a circle around her with her son at the foot of the bed, and her mother and daughter holding hands across the bed.

Around midnight, shortly before she transpired, she made eye contact with each one of the nine persons in the room. With our eyes locked, we said "Farewell," "God bless," and "Thank you for being!"

With the last exhalation she raised the corners of her lips as if to say, "It's wonderful, wonderful, wonderful."

Marion Commerford and Phyllis Ferris

From the Participatory Eulogy:
A Son's Commemoration

When speaking of Kay, many things can be said:
She was my mother, she was my friend.
Her intelligence was superior;
Her vocabulary astounding.
She was beautiful—inside and out.
Her strength is what impressed me the most.
Her inner vitality shone through her pain, and there were days when she glowed like the sun!
Radiance is what I called it.
Kay's greatest gift was her degree of caring.
She gave so much...
Farewell, Mother!
Thank you for sharing your Life and Light with us.

Michael Peterson

Kay's Memorial Garden

The idea of a memorial garden evolved during one of our talks. Kay was expressing how repugnant the practice of burial in cemeteries was to her. We talked about customs in other cultures and she stated that cremation with scattering of the ashes in the ocean would be her preference. She wondered, however, if that would deprive her family of a place to grieve and think of her. When I mentioned that such a place need not be the cemetery, but could be a garden, for instance, she absolutely lit up. "Kay's Memorial Garden! I love it," was her enthusiastic response. She became concerned about how and where this could be brought about, as money was in short supply.

I pointed out that this was not to be her concern. She was only to give her blessing to the garden idea. It would serve those who loved her well to be able to express their grief through action. It would give them comfort to do something in her memory. Creating a special place where they could go to remember her would be healing to the bereaved.

The garden idea found ready acceptance with her family and friends. Generous donations came to the Garden Chapel where her memorial service was held and where the garden was being considered.

The church's garden committee saw this as a great opportunity to make the grounds more inviting. During the following year, the family participated in planning and planting a lovely garden at the Garden Chapel.

On the anniversary of her death, Kay's Memorial Garden was formally dedicated:

To the Glory of God,
in honor of Kay,
in service to all who need a place of stillness
to restore their spirit.

It has become an oasis of tranquility in the midst of a bustling city. It is open to the public at all times as a place for contemplation and meditation—a fitting symbol for Kay's ecumenical spirit.

Inscribed on a plaque in Kay's Memorial Garden is Kay's favorite prayer, *A Simple Prayer*:

Lord, make me an instrument of your peace;
where there is hatred, let me sow love;
when there is injury, pardon;
where there is doubt, faith;
where there is despair, hope;
where there is darkness, light;
and where there is sadness, joy.

Grant that I may not so much seek to be consoled as to console;
to be understood, as to understand,
to be loved as to love;
for it is in giving
*   that we receive,*
it is in pardoning
*   that we are pardoned,*
and it is in dying
*   that we are born to eternal life.*

St. Francis

Epilogue

It is not you that is mortal, but only your body.
For that man whom your outward form reveals
Is not yourself; the spirit is the true self...
Cicero

Twenty-five years after my own adventure inward, described in the first chapter, and many life experiences richer, I feel I am ready to fulfill that perceived directive; namely, to help others lessen their fear of death and dying by sharing what I have learned.

In the intervening years since my initial experience beyond finite consciousness, the knowing that death is merely a portal that leads from limiting temporal existence to an expanded experience of life has grown even stronger. This knowledge was confirmed as I accompanied others who were preparing to make their transition from finite mortal life to immortal life. Some looked to the great adventure of "going home" with expectancy and peace—even joy—as demonstrated by Kay, for example.

This book was written for anyone who may be willing to consider death as a doorway one passes through when physical life comes to an end and new vistas on the continuum of consciousness open up.

BIBLIOGRAPHY

Cousins, Ewert, *World Spirituality: An Encyclopedic History of the Religious Quest*, Crossroads/Continuum Bulletin, 1985.

_____. *Christ of the 21st Century*, Rockport, MA: Element, Inc., 1992.

Dalai Lama, His Holiness the, *The Universe in a Single Atom: Convergence of Science & Spirituality*, New York: Broadway Publishing, 2006.

Frankl, Viktor, *Man's Search for Meaning*, New York: Washington Square Press, 1984.

_____. *The Doctor and the Soul*, New York: Vintage Books, 1986.

_____. *The Will to Meaning*. New York: Meridian, 1988.

_____. *Man's Search for Ultimate Meaning*, New York: Insight Books, 1997.

Gibran, Kahlil, *The Prophet*, New York: Alfred A. Knopf, 1970.

_____. *Sand and Foam*, New York: Knoft, 1926.

Graber, Ann V., *Viktor Frankl's Logotherapy: Method of Choice in Ecumenical Pastoral Psychology*, Lima, Ohio: Wyndham Hall Press, 2004 (2nd Edition).

_____. "Into the Spiral and Out," Twelve Gates to the City, *Chrysalis Reader*, vol. 2, 1996.

Hugo, Victor, from The Future Life, in *Current Literature: A Magazine of Record and Review*, vol. V (July-December, 1890), p. 129, New York: The Current Literature Publishing Co., retrieved October 23, 2009 from http://books.google.com

Jampolsky, Gerald, *Teach only Love*, New York: Bantam Books, 1983.

Kirven, Robert H., *A Book about Dying: Preparing for Eternal Life*, West Chester, PA: Chrysalis Books, 1997.

Knauer, Kelly (ed.) *Exploring the Unexplained: The World's Greatest Marvels, Mysteries and Myths*, New York: Time, Inc., 2006

Kübler-Ross, Elisabeth, *On Death and Dying*, New York: Macmillan Publishing Co., Inc., 1969.

_____. (Ed.). *Death: The Final Stage of Growth*, New Jersey: Prentice-Hall, 1975.

Lukas, Elisabeth, *Meaning in Suffering*, Berkeley, CA: Institute of Logotherapy Press, 1986.

Martin, Ernest, "The Last Days of Chester Buck" excerpted from Imagine That! Breaking through to Other Worlds, *Chrysalis Reader,* vol. 14, 2007.

Moore, Thomas, *Care of the Soul*, New York: Harper Collins, 1992.

Murasso, Jeremiah N., *Logotherapy and the Logos of God in Christic Wisdom*. Belleville, Ontario: Guardian Books, 2008.

Pietras, Penelope, Healing from Prenatal Loss, *The Messenger*, October, 1994.

Rienstra, David, Life's Blessings, *The Messenger*, February, 1997.

Shakespeare, William, *Romeo and Juliet*, (adapted from Act 3, Scene 2), online edition retrieved October 26, 2009 from http://gutenberg.org/etext/1112

Swedenborg, Emanuel, *Heaven and Hell* (Dole Translation). New York and West Chester, PA: Swedenborg Foundation, 1985.

Teilhard de Chardin, Pierre, *The Divine Milieu,* New York: Harper & Row, 1960.

_____. *The Future of Man*, New York: Harper and Row, 1964.

_____. *Toward the Future*, New York: Harcourt, 1975.

The Holy Bible, King James Version, Boston, MA: The Christian Science Publishing Society, 1990.

The Urantia Book, Chicago, IL: Urantia Foundation, 2000.

Yogananda, Pramahansa, *Autobiography of a Yogi*, Los Angeles, CA: Self-Realization Fellowship, 1983.

AUDIO-VIDEO RESOURCES

Frankl, Viktor, *Bewaeltigung der Vergaenglichkeit* (audio cassette). Innsbruck, Austria: Audiotex International, 1984.

Graber, Ann V. and Madsen, Mark, *Images of Transformation* (audio cassette album). Fountain Publishing, 1994.

Malone, Michael, *A Conversation with Viktor Frankl*, Videotape. (San Jose, KTEHSA Public Television), 1991.

Sadigh, Micah, *The Journey Home* (CD), Lovingston, VA: Monroe Products, 2004. Can be ordered directly from: micacd@ptd.net. Also available from: www.HemiSyncForYou.com/Monroe.

Shining Soul—Helen Keller's Spiritual Life and Legacy (DVD). Swedenborg Foundation, 2005.

INDEX

ACKNOWLEDGEMENTS

All Scripture quotations are from *The Holy Bible, King James Version*, Boston, MA: The Christian Science Publishing Society, 1990.

Pages 1–10: Chapter I: "Adventure Inward" by Ann V. Graber was first published under the title "Into the Spiral and Out" in *Twelve Gates to the City, A Chrysalis Reader, II,* © 1996 The Swedenborg Foundation. Variations have followed in other publications ("Ann's Story", *Chocolate for a Woman's Soul,* © 1997 Kay Allenbough, New York: Fireside Books, 1997).

Page 9: Teilhard de Chardin, Pierre, as quoted in Knauer, Kelly (ed.) *Exploring the Unexplained: The World's Greatest Marvels, Mysteries and Myths*, p. 90, © 2006 Time, Inc. Home Entertainment, 2006.

14: Malone, Michael, *A Conversation with Viktor Frankl*, Videotape, (San Jose, KTEHSA Public Television), 1991.

17: Frankl, Viktor, *Man's Search for Ultimate Meaning*, p. 151, © 1997 Plenum Press, New York: Insight Books, 1997.

20: His Holiness the Dalai Lama, *The Universe in a Single Atom: Convergenge of Science & Spirituality*, New York: Broadway Publishing, 2006.

23: Pierre Teilhard de Chardin, Pierre, *The Future of Man*, p. 244, Copyright © 1959 by Editions de Seuil, English translation © 1964, HarperCollins, All rights reserved, New York: Harper & Row, 1964.

24: Pascal, Blaise and Ariew, Roger (ed. and trans.), *Pensees*, p. 216, Copyright © 2004 Hackett Publishing Company, Inc., Indianapolis, IN: Hackett Publishing Company, 2005.

31: Lukas, Elizabeth, *Meaning in Suffering*, p. 68, ©1986 Institute of Logotherapy Press, Berkeley, CA: Institute of Logotherapy Press, 1986.

34: Jampolsky, Gerald, *Teach only Love: The Seven Principles of Attitudinal Healing*, © 1983 Gerald Jampolsky, New York: Bantam Books, 1983.

36: Teilhard de Chardin, Pierre, "The Evolution of Chastity" from *Toward the Future*, p. 86-87, Copyright © 1973 by Editions du Seuil, English translation © 1975 William Collins Sons & Co. Ltd and Harcourt, Inc, All rights reserved, New York: Harcourt, 1975.

49-51: "The Case of Father Joseph" previously published in *Viktor Frankl's Logotherapy: Method of Choice in Ecumenical Pastoral Psychology (2nd ed).* © 2003 Ann V. Graber, Wyndham Hall Press, 2004.

53: Quote by Gibran, Kahlil, *Sand and Foam,* © 1927 Kahlil Gibran, New York: Knopf, 1926.

54: Yogananda, Pramahansa, *Autobiography of a Yogi,* p. 377, © 1946 by Pramahansa Yogananda, © 1974 by Self-Realization Fellowship, Los Angeles, CA: Self-Realization Fellowship, 1983.

54–55: Cousins, Ewert, *Christ of the 21st Century,* Copyright © 1992 by Ewert H. Cousins, Rockport, MA: Element, Inc., 1992.

63: Shining Soul—Helen Keller's Spiritual Life and Legacy (DVD), © 2005 The Swedenborg Foundation, Swedenborg Foundation, 2005.

67: Frankl, Viktor, *The Will to Meaning,* p. 123, Copyright © 1969, 1988 by Viktor E. Frankl. All rights reserved. New York: Meridian, 1988. Frankl, Viktor, *Bewaeltigung der Vergaenglichkeit* (audio cassette), Innsbruck, Austria. Audiotex International, 1984. Translated by Ann V. Graber.

68: Kirven, Robert H., *A Book about Dying: Preparing for Eternal Life,* © 1997 Robert H. Kirven, West Chester, PA: Chrysalis Books, 1997.

75: Pietras, Penelope, "Healing from Prenatal Loss", *The Messenger,* October, 1994, © 1994 The Swedenborgian Church of North America.

77-78: Rienstra, David, "Life's Blessings", *The Messenger,* February, 1997. © 1997 The Swedenborgian Church of North America.

99: "A Simple Prayer," anonymous, credited to St. Francis, translated by Page, Kirby, *Living Courageously,* New York: Farrar & Rinehart, 1936. Originally published in French in *La Clochette,* n. 12, Dec. 1912, p. 285.

101: Cicero, as quoted in Knauer, Kelly *(ed.) Exploring the Unexplained: The World's Greatest Marvels, Mysteries and Myths,* p. 123, © 2006 Time, Inc. Home Entertainment, 2006.

Praise for *The Journey Home*

"*The Journey Home* uniquely combines and holds in creative tension the physiological and psychological dimensions of the dying process with the spiritual journey through death.... One of the great strengths of this book is that it... gives both a human and psycho-spiritual character that will appeal to both the layperson facing the reality of death, as well as the professional who is called upon to assist and minister to a dying person and their family."
The Very Rev. Philip C. Linder, D.Min., Psy.D.
Dean, Trinity Episcopal Cathedral, Columbia, SC

"Ann, your work is very special, I would say unique—as at the same time it is very spiritual, yet down-to-earth, concrete. Every chapter makes you see this transition from a different point of view. It is full of knowledge and understanding of life, full of luminous energy and power, bringing confidence to meet the unavoidable [death]. I would like to live through this book."
Mirja Kuutio, Helsinki, Finland

"After reading this phenomenal book, I began to evaluate my life and make decisions that were put on hold because of fear.... Perhaps I would not have made this decision to prepare myself for my own journey had I not read Dr. Graber's soul-inspiring manuscript."
Rosa M. Ramos, Elementary School Counselor

"Since reading this book, I have felt that there was finally some form of closure for my heart due to a very dear friend's death that had plagued me for the past three years.... However, all that changed for me the minute I began to turn the pages of the book.... It was such a profound experience that even as I flipped through the pages, I had tears streaming down my face as I read each sentence.

In addition, what I personally loved about this book was the ability of the author, Dr. Graber, to combine science and religion in discussing the one thing certain in this life, death. Most of the time, one hears the scientific explanation of death versus the religious and spiritual version of death, but not in this book. This book discusses death in a manner in which religion and science can co-exist."
Celina Castillo, Graduate Student

"*The Journey Home* could very well be that much-needed manual for both pastor and parishioner which —by removing the sting of death—provides comfort and reassurance to those preparing to die, those who care for them and those who live on....

Graber has lessened the fear of death through a vivid description of a remarkable and personal portrait of her experience with the dying process. Moreover, Graber has restored to death and to the dying process its *sacred dignity* by refocusing on man's spiritual origin as a return to and a fulfillment of a life's journey."
The Rev. Jeremiah N. Murasso, Ph.D., Ed.D.
Pastor, St. Francis of Assisi Church,
South Windsor,CT